Professional Acting in Television Commercials

Techniques, Exercises, Copy, and Storyboards

Pat Dougan

HEINEMANN
Portsmouth, NH

Heinemann
A division of Reed Elsevier Inc.
361 Hanover Street
Portsmouth, NH 03801–3912
Offices and agents throughout the world

Every effort has been made to contact copyright holders for permission to reprint borrowed material. We regret any oversights that may have occurred and would be happy to rectify them in future printings of this work.

The publisher is grateful to the following for permission to reprint previously published material:

p. 132–133 Tables from the 1990 and 1991 fall issues of *Screen Actor*, from the 1990 report, "The Female in Focus: In Whose Image?", and from the 1993 report, "Employment in Entertainment: The Search for Diversity." Reprinted courtesy of Screen Actors Guild.

Library of Congress Cataloging–in–Publication Data
Dougan, Pat
    Professional acting in television commercials: techniques, exercises, copy, and storyboards/by Pat Dougan.
      p. cm.
    ISBN 0–435–08659–6
    1. Acting for television—Vocational guidance. 2. Television advertising—Vocational guidance. I. Title.
PN1992.8.A3D68 1995
791.45′028′02373—dc20

94–33838
CIP

Acquisitions Editor: Lisa A. Barnett
Production Editor: J. B. Tranchemontagne
Cover Designer: Mary C. Cronin

Printed in the United States of America on acid–free paper
99 98 97 96 95 DO 9 8 7 6 5 4 3 2 1

Contents

Appendixes

Acknowledgments

So many people have been helpful to me while I wrote this book. People from all parts of the country, in all aspects of the business have shared their experiences, expertise, advice, headshots, resumes, commercial copy, and more. They include friends, actors, agents, casting directors, directors, union representatives, ad agency folks, and copywriters. Here they are.

Roslyn Arnstein
Steve Bautista
Douglass Bergmann
De Morge L. Brown
Rob Cain
Ann Chin
Ceoria Coates
Patty Collinge
Ellen Colton
Steve Connelly
Jim Cooke
Denise Cormier
Robert E. Cott, Jr.
Bill Cuccinello
Roger Curtis
Janis Dardaris
Harrise Davidson
Joan Debow
Dallas Derman
The DI Group

Nancy Doyle
Paul Dunn
Richard Fancy
Kevin Fennessy
Norma Fine
John Fiore
Jeff Garmel
Louise Goldenberg
Bill Goodell
Doug Goransson
Deborah Hopper
Carol Hurley
Carole R. Ingber
Gustave Johnson
Nancy Jordan
Tom Kemp
Roger Lateiner
Mark Locher
Marianne Maguire
Herb Mandell

David Marciano
Bill McCaw
Monique McIntyre
Cheryl McMahon
Bob Menahan
Eileen Michaels
Rodney Mitchell
Beverly Monchun
Wiley Moore
Patty Moran
Carrie Morgan
Carol Moss
Gary Moss
Sue Nichols
Jonathon Niles
Bob Owczarek
Erik Parillo
Dossy Peabody
Merle Perkins

Carolyn Pickman
Ronda Pierson
Nancy Politzer
Duncan Putney
M. Lynda Robinson
Harriet Rogers
Charles Rosen
Ellen Sargent
Timothy Sawyer
Dona Sommers
Ingrid Sonnichsen
Devon Sorvari
Jan Tallaksen
Meg Thalken
Maggie Trichon
Jack Welch
Ray Welch
Suzanne Whang
Fred Wilhelms

Advertising agencies and companies whose commercials appear in this book include:

Arnold Fortuna Lane
Blue Cross & Blue Shield
 of Massachusetts
Blue Cross & Blue Shield
 of Rhode Island
Cabot Advertising
Coca Cola USA
Creative Design & Marketing, Inc.
Drakes Bakeries
General Electric
General Electric Corporation
General Mills

Gillette
Helene Curtis
Ingalls, Quinn & Johnson
Ketchem Advertising
Key Corporation
Leo Burnett, USA
McCann-Erickson
New England Telephone
Ocean Spray
Panago Schenck & Kay
Polaroid
Saatchi & Saatchi
SmithKline Beecham

Great gratitude goes to my wonderful husband Mark Mason who is always supportive and patient. A very special thanks to my editor Lisa Barnett, who planted the seed in my mind to write this book. She supplied patience, encouragement, constructive comments, and a sense of humor. Thanks to J. B. Tranchemontagne for her creative ideas and collaborative spirit. Huge thanks to the reading committee—those folks who work in all areas of acting, directing, and/or commercials—for their insightful comments and very generous commitment of time: Stephanie Clayman, Danny Driscoll, Paul Horn, Peter Kovner, Larry Lane, Kathy Lubar, Paula Plum, and Maura Tighe. And finally, thanks to all my students who help me grow and keep me honest.

Introduction

Television commercial advertising in the United States is a huge industry. As early as 1950, 170 million dollars were spent on advertising for television. Later, in 1992 alone, over twenty-three *billion* dollars went to television advertising (*Advertising Age,* September 29, 1993). And the numbers continue to grow as they have over the past forty-three years.

How does this translate into acting jobs? During 1992, Screen Actors Guild actors earned $441 million dollars from television commercials, proving that commercials are still the bread and butter for today's actor.

This book will help you improve your on-camera skills and, I hope, your income. It is a step-by-step approach to the world of acting in television commercials. It covers, in a straightforward way, the details of on-camera acting techniques plus the nuts and bolts of the "business of the business," whether you are working in a big, medium, or small market. You will learn:

- on-camera techniques with real commercial copy for practice
- where to get training
- effective mental attitudes and techniques
- getting the best picture and resume
- audition etiquette
- how to dress
- how to design a marketing plan for yourself with or without an agent
- how to work with directors, casting directors, and agents
- earnings data

- where the jobs are
- union information

and much, much more.

Becoming proficient at acting in commercials takes time and practice. If you use the techniques and exercises in this book in sequence, I believe you will have the greatest success in developing or improving your skills. The appendixes have real commercial copy and storyboards for this purpose.

Whether you are a working professional, an actor making the crossover from theatre to on-camera work, or someone just beginning your acting career, I hope you will find this book informative and helpful.

On-Camera Versus Theatre Acting | 1

*I*n order to be a good on-camera actor, you must understand the *acting process* and have good acting techniques already in place. For these reasons, it's important to be theatre-trained. There is just no shortcut. Directors and agents want to feel confident that they are working with legitimate actors who have adequate training, flexibility, and skill to make the quick adjustments required for working in commercials. The internal acting process is the same whether you're working in commercials, theatre, or film.

How Is Acting in Commercials Different from Acting in the Theatre?

In most commercials your goal is to be natural, to be captured in a moment of "real" life.

- You *play yourself* rather than a character. Not so in the theatre. In commercials, you are chosen for your look, type, and skill. You play yourself in a given set of circumstances. There are some exceptions, of course, like the characters in the Tropicana Twister spots, Ocean Spray commercials, or Dunkin' Donuts ads. However, even if you're playing one of these characters, you don't have two or three weeks to develop a character as you would in the theatre.
- The *length* of commercials ranges anywhere from ten to sixty seconds. Unlike the theatre, you may be featured in as little as one or two seconds, or in the entire minute.

- The *size of the work* is much smaller, too, both vocally and physically, since you don't have to reach the back wall of the theatre. The size of the frame in commercials determines the size of your work. The smaller the frame, the smaller your facial expressions, gestures, volume, and movements. Recall those Citibank Visa commercials. We see a woman framed in a medium close-up, telling a quiet tale about how Citibank bailed her out in a cash emergency. She is very natural, with small expressions and little volume. The microphone is never more than six inches away, so she need only speak in a conversational tone.
- Successful commercials convey *a single thought or message.* The purpose of commercials is to make people aware of a particular product and persuade them to buy it. Obviously, plays have different goals although, like commercials, a play may have just one message to convey.
- *Earnings,* of course, represent another difference between commercials and stage work. You can make more money for one day's work in commercials than you can for a whole week of work in many theatres.

What Are the Similarities Between Acting in Commercials and the Theatre?

Just as in the theatre, in commercials *you must be a team player.* You work with a whole group of people including the director, assistant director, other actors, a cameraperson, a producer, a lighting person, a sound person, many crew members, and clients to make it all happen.

As in the theatre, *you need a driving, unshakable commitment and desire to get the work.* And as with theatre work, *you need to be trained.*

Training | 2

*T*he best on-camera actors are theatre-trained. Acting for the camera requires that you have an acting process in place. With proper theatre training and experience, you are ready to learn how to make effective adjustments to the smaller, more intimate, and "natural" medium, the camera. Also, training builds confidence.

Many theatre actors think that once they've done that one commercial, film, or corporate training film, they don't need to train for the camera. Learning to adjust your work to the camera takes time and practice—truthfully, years. You can learn through trial and error at auditions, or you can take classes. The best advice is to *keep training—even if you're working.* You'll just get better and better. The best actors continue to train and grow throughout their lives.

Larry Lane, the artistic director of a fine small theatre company, New Repertory Theatre in Boston, once said to me, "Acting is like a muscle. You have to keep exercising and working it to keep it in shape." And you keep growing the longer you work at it. Just look at the careers of some of the actors who have been in the business all their lives. You can see from their films how they've grown and gotten better over the years.

It is reported that when he's not working, Robert Duvall spends four hours a day working and studying film scripts on his own to improve his skills and keep tuned. Even brilliant actors continue to study and grow throughout their work lives. It is a lifelong journey. Remember, you will be competing with hundreds and sometimes thousands of other actors in your market who are already making money in the business. So the better the training you get, the more confidence you will have and the better your work will be.

What To Look For in On-Camera Training

There are two basic kinds of on-camera training: the acting class and private coaching. Coaching should be reserved for the professional who wants one-on-one help in focusing on a specific piece, a film role, or a commercial audition. You decide what you want to cover. Classes are the best way to learn new skills. There is simply no substitute for seeing yourself on-camera. It enables you to see what you're doing well and where you need improvement. You can also learn nearly as much from other students in a class as you can from watching yourself.

Find the Best Teacher

The main criteria in choosing any class should be the skills and reputation of the teacher and your feelings about him or her. What kind of a reputation does the teacher have among the *professional* acting community?

A teacher may have incredible acting and/or directing credits. You may know her wonderful work as an actor. But great actors may not be great or even good teachers. While it is critical that the teacher understand the process from the actor's point of view, you must determine each teacher's skills as a *teacher*. (Be aware that a great acting teacher is not necessarily a good coach.)

How Well Does the Teacher Know the Acting Business and Current Trends?

Is the teacher a working actor herself? A teacher may advertise that she has been in the business for twenty years. Yet that person may not have *worked* in the business for the last ten years. She may be out of touch with the industry as it exists today. On the other hand, even without having worked in the industry in the last ten years, a teacher may have kept current with the industry by understanding the changes in commercial styles and updating her teaching accordingly. You have to evaluate this.

Trust your feelings about the teacher. You spend a good deal of time opening up emotionally in acting classes. You want to feel safe and free to take chances. So your impressions and feelings about the teacher are important. Working as closely and honestly as you will with your teacher, you'll want to like her.

But remember that acting teachers (or coaches) are not therapists or gurus. Sympathetic, yes, but they're not there to help you with a breakup with your lover. Certainly they should be supportive, challenging, and helpful. But they are humans like you and me. So don't expect God.

Where to Look for a Great Teacher

How do you find a great teacher? Good on-camera teachers can be found teaching either privately or through professional acting schools. To determine the skill of the teacher, check with a variety of sources including actors, casting directors, and agents.

OTHER ACTORS

Many actors may say they have heard so-and-so is a great teacher but they have not actually studied with that teacher. Talk to working professionals who have studied with a variety of teachers. Ask your actor friends to describe what they liked about the teacher and the class and what they didn't like.

Before students sign up for my class, I advise them to talk to two or three of my previous students and really quiz them on what they learned, how the students were treated, how I compare to other teachers and classes, and so forth. Any good acting teacher should be willing to do this.

If you are seriously interested in a particular teacher, ask to audit or sit in on one class. What is his or her teaching style? How does he work with the students? Do his exercises lead to good results? What are your impressions overall? A good teacher should offer either a free introductory session or the opportunity for a potential student to sit in and observe one class.

CASTING DIRECTORS AND AGENTS

Casting directors and agents can also be a great source of recommendations. Keep in mind that they hear who is good in the industry and naturally want to send actors to good teachers. Try calling a reputable casting director (CD) or agent's office and ask the receptionist, "Does your agency recommend any outstanding commercial acting classes or teachers?" The purpose of the call is to get teacher/class information, not to seek an audition. But don't sign up before checking out the teacher yourself. Make it a point to audit or sit in on a class first.

Many casting directors themselves teach acting classes, either independently or through acting schools. Some feel this is a conflict of interest because it implies preferential casting treatment for those who take classes. You may choose to take a class to be seen by one of these folks, but be aware that there is no guarantee that you will be cast. If a particular casting director is reputed to be the best acting *teacher* in town, however, go for it. The bottom line always is to find the best *teacher*.

SCHOOLS AND STUDIOS

There are a variety of schools and studios, some good, some bad, who offer commercial acting classes. Good and bad reputations spread by word of mouth. Good teachers don't work at bad schools. The best sources of information on classes in schools are your working actor friends. Certainly, casting directors and agents will also *hear* who is good, but actors will have studied with the good teachers.

Does the studio or school turn out working actors? Are its alumni earning money in the business? Are its fees in line with other reputable classes? Are they willing to let you audit one class? Will they give you names of students who have studied there? The school or studio may have some big names attached to it. But the *quality of the teacher* is the issue.

Avoid teachers or schools who focus on something other than acting, like EST or religion or group therapy. These studies may be fine, but they should not be the focus of a professional acting class.

TRADE PAPERS

If you just can't get any good ideas from people in the industry, ask yourself why not. Read through some of the actors' trade papers or publications in your area, and then ask the teacher to send you a brochure or flyer. If after you have read the material you are interested in the class, ask to audit one session and interview the teacher.

Don't be swayed by the quality of the brochure or flyer a teacher or school is printing. A slick, high-quality brochure or flyer is no guarantee of a high-quality teacher or school.

What to Ask a Prospective Teacher

Here are some questions to ask when interviewing a teacher.

- What material is covered in the class? (On-camera techniques, character development, audition conduct, script analysis, self-marketing?)
- How is each class period structured? (Amount of on-camera time versus lecture?)
- Does everyone get on-camera time during each class?
- What kinds of commercials will we work on? (Spokesperson, slice-of-life, improvisation, two or more people in dialogue?)
- What kinds of homework are required or suggested between classes?
- Do you provide written materials to supplement your teaching?
- What is the length of the class? (Days and hours per week? How many weeks?)
- What is the average size of your class?

- What is the level of experience of the other students in the class? (I try to match experience levels: beginners with beginners, intermediates with the same, and so on.)
- Is an audition required?
- What is your particular style of teaching? Are you tough, challenging, easygoing, abusive (forget it!)?
- How long have you been teaching?
- Do you teach only, or do you also act? (Try to get the teacher to talk about the range of her career. Most teachers are better if they have acted.)
- Will the class be auditioned by a director or producer or casting person at the end?
- What is the fee? When is it payable?
- What is your refund and cancellation policy?
- Would you give me two or three names of your past students I can talk to?
- May I audit one class?

Some teachers offer that at the end of the class you will be critiqued by some well-known casting person or director. Although it is worthwhile to be seen by one of these people, this should not be the only benefit you get from the class. The teacher should stand on his own. His skills should be significant with or without the visiting casting person.

You may have other questions that are important to you. Use this as a guide. Do not be afraid to ask tough questions. You are the consumer. You are buying the skills and services of the teacher.

Questions to Ask Other Actors

Here are also some suggestions for questions to ask your actor friends who have studied with a teacher you are interested in. Most of these questions can also be asked about a coach.

- Did he have clear concepts?
- Did he give clear "process" directions?
- Did his exercises work for you and others?
- What was his process to get a particular result?
- What did you especially like about him and the class?
- What didn't you like?
- How was the class environment? Did it feel like a safe place in which to experiment?
- Did you like the way he worked with you and others?
- How did he treat people? Was he supportive, constructive, abusive, and so forth? (Did you like his style?)
- Do you feel you have gained skills, confidence, knowledge?

- Specifically, what did you learn?
- What techniques or lessons did you come away with?
- Would you study with him again?

There are a lot of people claiming to be teachers out there. In the final analysis, the three most important factors in choosing a great acting teacher are the teacher's skills, his/her reputation among working actors and other professionals in the industry, and your feelings about the person. With a little investigation, you're bound to find the best teacher or coach for you.

Mental Tools | 3

*I*t is just as important to be mentally prepared for a career in acting as it is to perfect your acting and self-marketing skills. There are a number of mental and psychological tools that can make it easier for you. They include building confidence, practicing, never apologizing for your work, being persistent and likable, and handling rejection. There are some concerns you may have, too, like nervousness, or losing self-esteem. Fortunately, there are positive ways to conquer these problems. First, let's talk about the importance of practicing.

Practice

No matter how many classes you take, it's important to practice. As with any art form, you must perfect the technical skills. And it takes time. Classes can teach you the basics. But in order to compete by auditioning and winning roles, you must practice. Through practice, you will become adept at making strong and varied choices in your work, both at auditions and on the job.

Practice while you're taking classes, with friends, at home in front of the mirror, or with a video camera. Practice builds confidence. Practice makes perfect, (well, close maybe). Even after you have the basic on-camera skills, practice, practice, practice!

Confidence

No matter who you are, it is very difficult to feel confident when learning new techniques. There is no shortcut to confidence. Once you have the skills to do the work, you begin to feel a bit of confidence. When you start auditioning and feeling good about your work, whether or not you get the job, your confidence builds. (Remember, based on the odds, it's impossible to get all the jobs.) As you begin to win some of the auditions and shoot commercials, you feel more and more confident and able to do the work.

The more you practice, audition, and work, the more confident you will feel. It all takes time, so have patience with yourself. It won't do any good to beat yourself up. That will destroy your confidence.

As actors, we are often in powerless positions. Someone else has the power to call us in to audition. Someone else has the power to choose us for the job. Someone else directs us in the commercial. An actor can end up feeling out of control and vulnerable. An actor can end up feeling that she's not worth much unless she's hired for a job. Try this on for size: "I am a whole, good person whether or not I am hired for this job." It is critical that you feel whole with or without acting. If your self-worth and self-esteem are being determined largely by someone you barely know who happens to have the power to hire you at this particular moment, you will find it very difficult to feel peace or confidence in yourself in this business.

To do good work as actors, we need to be vulnerable and emotionally accessible. It is also very important to find a way to protect ourselves from the non-acting parts of the business like rejection, the politics, and the business aspects. We need to be able to find that balance so that we are whole people, no matter what business we're in.

About Nerves

Everyone gets nervous at some time while doing an audition or shooting a commercial, television show, film, soap, or corporate video. You may start thinking, "Why am I so nervous? What's wrong with me? Nobody else is as nervous as I am." The fact of the matter is *everyone* gets nervous sometimes. It's normal. Nerves are usually greater with a person who lacks skills or confidence or with someone who is trying to be perfect. The question is *not* how to get rid of the nerves, but rather how to accept them, adapt to them, and live with them.

Here are some hints. First of all, as you get more experience on-camera, your level of nervousness will subside. Think about the first time you drove a car or rode a bicycle. You were probably a nervous wreck. But now you can do both practically without thinking. It's completely automatic.

A physical warm-up always helps. Before your audition do some vocal sighs, some physical loosening-up exercises, such as jumping up and down with your body limp as a rag. Take some slow, deep breaths to slow down your pounding heart. Or have a good laugh. Force yourself to laugh about something. You may have to force it, but it *will* lighten up your mood and fears. Then give yourself time enough to get composed before you walk into the audition. Do not go in gasping for breath.

Share your nervousness with someone else who seems nervous. If you don't know anyone at the audition or job, look around. You're bound to see someone who looks afraid. Strike up a conversation with the person, and say this is your first, or second, or tenth audition and you're nervous. Usually, the person will be relieved that someone else is nervous, too. However, keep in mind that actors are there to audition. Respect their need to prepare. And don't *expect* another person to make you feel better.

Try accepting and making friends with your nerves. "Hi, nerves. Yup, you've got me today. Well, how are you? We're going to work together today as a team. I'll respect you and you keep me on my toes."

Finally, lay off the caffeine. It increases your heart rate.

I have suffered from pretty bad anxiety attacks during performances in my life. It's been helpful for me to know that the nervousness and anxiety are not necessarily about the work. They're usually about something else that's going on in my life, and they tend to come up when I'm feeling most vulnerable and unprotected. Let me share a personal anxiety story with you.

Early in my career, while I was becoming established as an on-camera actor, I was also working in voice-overs. I was called in to do a radio spot for a large newspaper. Their regular voice-over actor was out of town on vacation.

One aspect of the voice-over business that used to bother me was the lack of interaction when you're in the sound booth and the producer and client are in the studio. You're in there reading the copy, and you look up and see them talking and waving their hands around and making faces. But you can't hear what they're saying. It's tempting to think they're talking about what you might be doing wrong, and you start to get paranoid and lose confidence. Naturally, you're sure they're saying, "God, she's awful. Can't she do it right? I don't know if we can get what we need from her for this." Chances are they aren't. (If there's one thing I've learned in this business, it's that producers, directors, and clients (a) may not be clear about what they are looking for in the spot so they need to talk about it and develop it, or (b) may know what they want but don't know how to communicate it.)

Anyway, I go in to do this radio spot and I am already afraid since I'm intimidated by this really great actor I'm replacing. This was a sixty-second spot with a music bed underneath so it had to be done all in sixty seconds with no possibility of pickups in case of errors. Plus the ad agency producer was the worst kind, who thought of actors as mere machines, without feelings, to be used to crank out copy.

During the session, the producer, while piling on too many directions to incorporate all at once, got verbally abusive, saying things that confirmed my worst fears about my abilities. I had an anxiety attack while I was reading the voice-over. I couldn't focus on the work. I felt totally trapped. I was certain I would never get the spot done. Doing that sixty-second spot seemed like a lifetime in hell to me. And at that moment it was.

To this day when I do a voice-over, I pump myself up with positive thought and the acknowledgment that I will be nervous. I have accepted the nervousness (some days better than others), which tends to lessen the anxiety and nervousness. After this many years in the business, (a) I know I am not going to die from nervousness or anxiety; (b) if I acknowledge it and take some deep breaths, my heart rate decreases although I may still be nervous; (c) I say to myself, "Yes! I can do this, just as I have hundreds of times before!" rather than, "Oh, God, I'm scared. I feel awful. I don't want to do this." This way I'm choosing to go with the positive possibilities rather than sinking into the fear. (This sometimes works and sometimes doesn't.) And (d), I focus on my purpose (developing the character, playing the action of the spot, reacting to the other characters, and so forth). I try very hard not to push the nervousness away or beat myself up, both of which make me feel worse and more nervous. All of this is what I call "being with the nervousness."

From this very painful early experience, I learned that nothing is worth being treated like a dog. Acting is a job. I do it not only to feed my creative soul but also to pay the rent. I learned not to give away my personal power or self-esteem to anyone, particularly someone I don't know who happens to have a *single* opinion. Of course, I always work at being open and flexible in my work, but only to a point. No one has the right to be abusive—*no one.*

Remember, when you're nervous, that it's only an audition or a one-day job. It's not the end of the world. They can always do another take if need be. You can also ask to take a break, and get some water. Try to lighten up. Laugh. And breathe. You will not die from being nervous!

I listened to that radio spot later. It sounded good. I even used it on an early voice-over reel. I was the only one on that job who knew of my anxieties. What I learned from it was that despite my anxieties, I was much better than I thought.

Apologies

No matter what, *never apologize for your work* at an audition or on the job, either visually or verbally, even if you feel you did a lousy job. Many people who are starting out comment on their audition or work after a take by saying, "Oh, God, I'm really sorry. That wasn't very good. Can I do it again?" Or they will roll their eyes skyward as if to say, "Boy, that stunk. I'm so glad that's over." Of course all of this is heard or seen on-camera by the producer, client, casting director, or director, and any good impression you've made is immediately thrown out the window. They may have thought your audition was good until you apologized. You may *feel* like apologizing; you may be *thinking* of apologizing, but don't show it or say it. *Never, never* apologize for your work.

If you feel you did a lousy first take at an audition, ask for another shot at it. You can say, "Could I try that again?" which may or may not get you another chance. On the job, there is nearly always room for additional takes. If you feel you haven't done your best, frame your request in a positive way with confidence, and say something like "I'd like to try that a different way. Can we do it once more?" This is not an apology, but rather a personal artistic challenge, and a businesslike approach.

The simplest and, indeed, the only way to change a bad habit like apologizing is to make a conscious decision to change it. Make a deliberate mental note that you are beginning to end the habit. Say it out loud. Don't try to end several bad habits all at once. Begin with one at a time. When you've succeeded with the first one, move on to the next. And be nice to yourself. You won't change the habit overnight. It all takes time.

Protective Covers

It's a very delicate balance to be artistically open and adaptable in your work and at the same time protect yourself from the rejection and other cruelties of the business. Actors have ways of protecting themselves from being too vulnerable in their work. This sometimes takes the form of putting up a wall or barrier that keeps the real person from showing through. This is what I call the actor's protective cover.

Although this protective cover can help you feel safer or more in control in a given moment (particularly when you're nervous or when you're working with a nasty person), it can prevent you from doing your best work.

Protective covers come in many forms: defensiveness, laughing at inappropriate times, never smiling, acting tough or overconfident, an overly blasé attitude—you name it. Whatever shape a cover takes, it prevents you from really connecting in your work. We all have a protective cover at some time, usually early on in our work.

How do you identify your protective cover? If you are working with a good teacher, he will be able to help you identify it and get rid of it. *You* have to be aware of it and see it *yourself* to begin to get rid of it. You have to acknowledge that it *is* a protective cover, that it stands in the way of your work really connecting. You have to respect and trust your on-camera teacher when he points it out. Your work will be more honest, connected, and "in the moment" when you can identify and acknowledge the cover and then give it up .

Rejection

The world of acting is constant rejection. Selection is an integral part of the business since there are always more actors than jobs. When we are rejected, we tend to take it personally. It's a natural response. We might think, "They don't like me. I must not be any good. Oh, God, what's the matter with me?"

Rejection is a given in the acting business. You will spend more time being rejected than almost anything else except, perhaps, marketing yourself. I know this may sound silly, but you can't take it personally. You can't afford to. It's true. The more you know about the commercial acting business, the more you will learn that casting is primarily based on "type" for a particular commercial. In the larger markets, you'll notice that pretty much everyone competing with you looks alike; that is, same hair color, same age range, same kind of character. You know for a fact that there is only one actor who can be hired for that role. So assuming all ten of you have similar skills, a simple calculation will tell you that your odds are one in ten of getting the job. The client may have liked one actor's hairdo better than the others. He may have liked one of the others' interpretive choices more than yours, *even though you made good choices.* Someone else may have looked more like the character on the storyboard than the others. Maybe the casting director was sick that day and lost focus after the first two auditions. It could be anything.

Also, commercials are cast by committee, never by one person. There's the client, ad agency people, casting director, and the director. It's a group decision. You may be brilliant, but unless you match the individual criteria of each committee member—look, type, skill, ability to take direction—you may not win that job. Then again, you may. You just never know. It's all a crapshoot.

Of course, you have to keep your skills tuned and be able to take direction effectively at a moment's notice. These two variables clearly increase your odds of winning jobs. You may find it helpful to keep track of your auditions and jobs and compare them with the data of other actors of your age and type. I keep a date book that lists the dates and times of my auditions, who called me to audition, the product or client, the kind of job (commercial, industrial, voice-over, and so on), and if I booked the job. Every three months I take a look at these data to see how I'm doing. If I have auditioned five or more times without booking a job, I think about it. (This average will vary widely depending on your market and type.) Did they cast it younger? Did they go with a brunette? Did I have an attitude that day? Did my work feel off balance? Were my stakes high enough? This kind of tracking may help you see patterns and determine where you might need to focus more attention in your work to increase your odds of booking jobs. If nothing else, it's revealing information.

You do not want to get in the habit of blaming yourself when you don't get a job. This is not to say you should not evaluate your work after an audition or job, but beating yourself up won't improve your work or your attitude. It will just keep you stuck in the dumps.

Rejection is a given. It is a constant and continual fact of life in the acting business. *If you cannot seriously accept rejection and live with it, you may want to rethink your career choices now.* As Michael Shurtleff, author of that wonderful book *Audition,* said, "If there is anything else you want to do, do it" (*StageSource News,* Boston, January/February 1993, volume 8, number 3, page 12).

Persistence

In most careers, once you have proven skills and earned a good reputation, you can pull back a bit and concentrate primarily on your work. Not so in the acting business. Your skills and good reputation may get you the auditions, but you still have to audition for nearly every job throughout your career.

Commercial acting involves a never-ending self-marketing plan. If you are in a market where everyone has an agent, you may think your job is done. But even with an agent you must make sure she's working to get you work. Remember, agents have lots of actors to keep employed.

If you live in a market where there are no agents, you must be your own agent. And there is no end to the number of contacts that you, as a freelancer, can pursue and maintain.

You must be hungry for the work, either psychologically or literally, to persist in the face of the odds and rejection. And you must be able to maintain that persistence and drive over the course of your career, which I hope will be many, many years.

The *Random House College Dictionary* defines "persist": "to continue steadily or firmly in some state, purpose, or course of action in spite of opposition; to stand firm permanently." Can you be persistent in pursuing your acting career for ten, fifteen, or twenty years? It's a good question to ask yourself.

Being Likable

In an all too unpredictable and crazy business, even with all the proper skills, if you are a positive and likable person you will get farther. Being likable does not, of course, mean being a pushover. It means being friendly, easy to get along with, and flexible for the good of the project.

Throughout my career, I have auditioned and worked with people who didn't have the best skills or talent, and yet because they were nice and easy to work with, they were sometimes chosen over those with more skills but less likable personalities, or *prima donnas.*

I have a friend who was a major on-camera talent. He was very big in the business and always worked a lot. At one point, however, his "fame" went to his head and he became rather demanding and sometimes unpleasant on the job. He treated a casting assistant and some crew members as if they were there to serve him. Eventually, this casting assistant became a casting director and remembered this treatment. Needless to say, this actor was never called again by this casting director. The actor still has a reputation of being difficult even though his attitude has improved. It takes a long time to turn around a bad reputation.

It's important to be likable and friendly to everyone *in this business,* not just the agent, casting director, client, or director. Today's secretary may be tomorrow's casting director; today's grip can be tomorrow's director. Being a likable person still carries the day, in this business and any other. Remember: your reputation will precede you.

Physical Tools | *4*

*T*raining and mental tools are part of the puzzle. Then come the essential physical tools: headshots, resumes, postcards, answering services, and demo reels, which you need to be a serious player in this business.

- You need a great headshot and resume because they are your business card and your most important marketing tools.
- You must have a reliable telephone answering machine, answering service, voice mail, or service.
- You need a variety of appropriate wardrobe choices for auditions.
- Postcards and demo reels of your commercial work are additional marketing tools that are extremely useful.

Remember, you are in an outrageously competitive business. You're vying for too few jobs with too many already established actors. All your marketing pieces must look interesting, professional, and classy, as good as or better than what's already out there!

Getting a Great Headshot

I have seen thousands of headshots over the years, some good, some bad, few great. Getting a great headshot requires two things: a clear understanding of what is needed, and proper preparation.

The first consideration is: *what are the requirements in your market?* In the larger markets like New York, Los Angeles, and Chicago, you use a commercial headshot only for commercial auditions. In medium-sized and smaller markets actors may use their commercial headshot for all their on-camera work. Will a commercial headshot be sufficient in your market for all your on-camera auditions? You must determine the norm in your market. Be clear about how you intend to use your commercial headshot before you start interviewing photographers. If you decide to get several kinds of shots—commercial, legit, or portrait, for example— be clear in your own mind and with the photographer beforehand.

The second requirement is to *be adequately prepared before having your picture taken.* It takes plenty of planning and several attempts before you get a really great headshot. As in all businesses, you must do your homework and know what is expected of both you and the photographer before you proceed. Unfortunately, some actors are so eager to get started that they run out and have a quick picture taken before they understand exactly what they need.

Why waste your time and money when you're just going to have to go out and repeat the process? Let's be clear: do not go out and have your pictures taken until you understand what you need.

Your headshot and resume are your sales brochure, and you are the product. In order to contend in this highly competitive business, your headshot and resume need to be your own special piece of artwork, as good as or better than those currently in the market. If they are mediocre or bad, you probably won't even get called in for the audition.

Every marketing aspect of your acting business has to look completely professional. If you start out with a so-so picture and resume, it will take you years to recover from the damage. Although not all casting directors or agents remember everybody's bad picture and resume, if they remember yours, you are doomed. You'll spend the next several years trying to prove that you're not really an amateur. Obviously, spending time and money compensating for earlier bad judgments takes valuable time away from the task at hand, getting work.

THE COMMERCIAL HEADSHOT STYLE

The best kind of headshot for commercial work is warm, friendly, energetic, and inviting. It should capture your real personality. Your body should be squarely facing the camera. Eyes are very important. Your eyes must make a connection with that person in the camera. You should be looking directly at the camera and actively inviting the viewer into your space by playing an action each and every time the camera clicks. You should choose and play actions in your still photography session just the way you do in your on-camera work.

The style of a commercial headshot is distinct from the style of a legit (theatre/film, soap opera, or corporate video) headshot. The commercial headshot should have these qualities:

- Warm, friendly, inviting, energetic, and open
- Look exactly like you—a "put-together" you
- Eyes that are active and smiling, making a connection with the camera
- Actor smiling with teeth showing
- Excellent technical qualities:
  - Sharp skin tones, not an airbrushed look
  - Evenly lit—we want to see your whole face in light
  - Proper contrast between you and the background
- Clothes should enhance, not stand out
- No posing and no jewelry

Portrait or three-quarter shots are popular in Los Angeles and in some of the other markets for both commercials and legit work. Although they are used in New York as well, they are losing popularity at this writing. The portrait shot is a more relaxed and casual likeness of you. It is a bit freer in style than the headshot. It is framed wider than your head, down to your waist or knees. You are more physically relaxed, and dressed in clothing typical of your everyday life. Denim is prevalent.

In certain markets portrait shots are used for everything. Some casting directors feel portrait shots capture the actor's personality and physical appearance better than headshots. Sometimes actors have two or more different shots: one warm and friendly for commercials, a friendly business look for corporate videos, one more thoughtful and contemplative for film and theatre work, and sometimes a fourth for soap operas, which is more glamorous, upscale and alluring or provocative. (These categories are the same in headshot styles, too.)

Most casting directors still prefer to see a good headshot for commercial work. Whatever your choice, *your picture should look exactly like you.* When you go to a casting session, you should look as if you just stepped out of the picture. You are being called in because the client likes what she sees in your picture and wants to see that same person walk into the casting session.

Capturing the real you means wrinkles, freckles, and all. You will not be able to remove these in real life, so your headshot should also show them. As long as you look natural in real life, you can use makeup for toning down these "defects" in your headshot.

You must be able to see the texture of your skin in your headshot. You are not going to look airbrushed at the audition, nor should you in your headshot. (In New York, airbrushed and a bit more glamorous than "natural" is the norm.) However, remember—your appearance should not surprise the casting director.

CHOOSING A PHOTOGRAPHER

Now that you've decided what is needed, it's time to choose a photographer. You want to find one who does commercial headshots as a specialty. Some photographers do all kinds of actors' pictures well, some don't. You will need to determine this from their portfolios. Remember, a photographer who takes pictures for theatrical productions, family portraits, dance companies, or ads for magazines probably does not have the skills of a photographer who specializes in actors' headshots.

Many of the first-time headshots I've seen look as if they were taken by the actor's significant other. The actor is standing by her apartment building or next to a tree. The friend may be an excellent photographer. But does the person *specialize* in headshots? If not, please save yourself time, money, and reputation, and find an excellent professional photographer who specializes in actors' headshots.

Once you've asked friends for recommendations and done your own research, choose at least three photographers to interview.

INTERVIEWING THE PHOTOGRAPHERS

You can do the interviews over the phone. Here are some questions to ask:

- Do you specialize in commercial headshots?
- Do you take other kinds of acting shots (theatre, film, soaps)?
- Can you take both styles in the same session?
- How many rolls do you take? How many shots?
- What do you charge? Exactly what does your fee include?
- Does your fee include any finished 8 × 10s?
- How much are additional finished 8 × 10s?
- Who keeps the negatives, you or me?
- Do you work with a hair and makeup stylist and is that included in the fee?
- If not, do you recommend a stylist?
- If the stylist's fee is extra, what does she charge?
- What is your technique for working with the actor in terms of capturing the actor with active thoughts?
- Do you guarantee your work? What about retakes if I'm not satisfied? Is there an additional charge?
- What are your suggestions for clothing color and type?
- How far in advance would I need to schedule a session?
- How long does it take to get the contact sheets after the shoot?
- How long to get the final 8 × 10s?
- What production house(s) do you recommend for reproducing quantities?
- May I make an appointment to see your portfolio?

You may have other questions as well, but these will give you a good start.

JUDGING THE PORTFOLIOS

Look at portfolios to decide which photographer's work you like best. In the photographer's work, you should see all the elements we've discussed for getting a great headshot. Keep looking at portfolios until you are satisfied. Don't settle for less. It is also helpful if you like the photographer, since you want to feel comfortable working with him.

Actress Stephanie Clayman, who has worked in the Boston, New York, and Los Angeles markets, gives this piece of advice, especially to young actors: "It's essential that you feel relaxed and comfortable with your photographer. Often I look at headshots, and the main expression in the eyes is one of sheer terror. Don't let the photographer intimidate you. You're paying for the session. He's working for you, not the other way around."

TAILORING YOUR LOOK

If you're already working as a commercial actor, you will have fine-tuned your look. If you need to make adjustments before your photo session, check out how people in your age range and type look and dress in TV commercials. How are they cast? What are they wearing? How is their hair styled? Another resource is other actors already in the business. It's valuable to keep up with changing trends. What are the top actors in your market and type wearing, both in their headshots and on the job? How is their hair styled?

More and more we see "real" people in commercials. There was a time when all the people in ads had blond hair and looked as if they came from Iowa or southern California. Trends and looks change with the years and the markets, so it's important to keep up with what's happening now.

CLOTHING

Keep in mind that your clothing should augment rather than stand out in your headshot. The best choices are classic casual, "put-together" casual, not messy or worn out. Ask your photographer for suggestions about fabric and colors. Keep in mind that dark colors photograph as black—which can look dramatic. Light colors often provide no contrast at all.

HAIR

How should you wear your hair? Again, watch TV. Your hair should resemble that of other people in commercials in your type and age range. *For women, a simple, classic cut is best, as long as you are middle-of-the-road.* If you are a teenager, notice what the young women are wearing for cuts. Often younger women and girls can have slightly longer than shoulder-length hair. But be sure to watch commercials and see if that is still the case. As I have mentioned before, trends change from year to year. But it is always safe to be middle-of-the-road.

If you color your hair, make sure it doesn't look it. We don't want to see your roots.

Men should also wear their hair neat and contemporary. At this writing, long hair and ponytails are quite popular for men again. However, you *rarely* see this style on men in commercials. You see it in TV series and films, but seldom in commercials. Likewise, beards and mustaches are generally a no-no.

Find a good hair stylist to cut and *maintain* your hair. It is vital to find a hair stylist who works with on-camera actors. If you are planning a new hairstyle, live with it for three or four weeks before having your new headshots taken. This gives you time to work out any changes or kinks or adjustments.

MAKEUP

Your makeup should look natural and enhance your look. It should not stand out or be the focal point of the picture.

If you are comfortable doing your own makeup for black and white, great. If you are not, you will want to consider using a stylist. This way, *you* won't have to worry about your makeup and hair during the shoot.

Men, if you have heavy beard shadows, be sure to shave before the session. You may need a light application of makeup base or powder.

The bottom line is your makeup should look natural, to highlight and enhance your features. You should look like you.

JEWELRY

Here's an easy one that requires no homework. *Don't wear any jewelry. None, nada, zip!* Nothing. Now, some of you aren't going to follow this, I know. You will see some actor in a headshot with something on, stud earrings or something. Well, I'm not making this up. The casting directors and agents prefer no jewelry in your commercial headshot. They don't want to see your jewelry. They want to see *you!* Give 'em what they want and improve your chances of getting in the door.

GLASSES

As you watch TV, you'll notice a lot of people wearing glasses these days. They have become a fashion statement: business people, scholarly types, students of all ages, "intelligent" people, grandparents, character types. You'll see glasses worn in commercials, too.

If you have them and they seem appropriate for your type, you may want to try a few shots with glasses. (To prevent glare, pop out the lenses in your glasses before the session.) However, you definitely need to be able to work without them. If you need glasses, please get contacts as an option.

Remember, commercials are intended to reflect the majority of real people in real-life situations, so make sure *all* your choices contribute to that knowledge. Again, watch TV. That's where you will find most of the answers.

The point of all this detail is to end up with a *great* picture. A lot of this may seem tedious. And you could go on planning forever and never get the damned picture taken. Naturally, I'm not suggesting that. What I'm saying is: make it look great!

AT THE SHOOT

Here are some reminders for the shoot itself. As I've said, a good head-shot should capture you actively making a connection with that one person in the camera. Some photographers have particular techniques to help you relax, look natural, and be spontaneous and energetic for each click of the camera. They may suggest you relax your smile between each shot. Or turn your head away from the camera, turn back and say, "Come here," "Yes!," "Show me!" or "Hi!" as the picture is taken. It's a good idea to come prepared with some of your own techniques for maintaining an active and spontaneous connection with the camera. Don't expect the photographer to inspire you.

- Don't put your hands in the picture.
- Keep your head straight up and down, square to the camera.
- *Show your teeth* when you smile. The best headshots capture the actor at the peak of his smile. Not at the beginning or on the way down, but at the highest point of the smile.
- Don't pose. If you are really playing actions, you won't be posing.
- Wiggle your face around between shots to keep it loose and spontaneous.
- Be prepared to repeat the same actions, as if for the first time, each time, click after click of the camera.
- Relax, yet stay alive. It's just like working in film or on tape: still cameras capture everything.

COST

How much can you expect your photo session to cost? Plan to spend between $125 and $600 for the photo session alone, which may or may not include a stylist and one or more finished prints.

THE CONTACT SHEET AND FINAL PRINTS

If you're lucky, you will have the problem of too many good choices. Use a photographer's loupe to look at your contact sheet. The rule of thumb is: *never choose your own pictures.* Actors tend to choose the pictures that make them look better or more glamorous than they are in real life. Of course, you will want to make some preliminary selections. Then it is best to get two or three professional opinions before you make your final choice.

Whose opinions should you seek? The people who call you in: casting directors and agents. You may also ask another working actor whose opinion you respect.

For your final selection, you may want to limit yourself to three or four 8 x 10s. Some originals may look a bit out of focus when enlarged. Some of the skin tones may not be as sharp as they looked on the contact sheets. Maybe your expression isn't as effective as it looked in the smaller shots. Each finished print can cost $8 to $15, in addition to your session fee. If you need to have more originals made because of dissatisfaction with the first round, it can run into money.

Many reproduction houses will print 5 × 7s for you. It's an excellent way to preview shots you're not quite sure about, and it's cheaper than 8 × 10s. Of course, once you make your selections, the final reproductions will be 8 × 10s.

If you judge your final prints to be unacceptable because of poor technical quality, discuss this with the photographer. You don't want to end up settling for something you're truly unhappy with and can't feel good about sending out. He may need to do some final prints for free, or you may have to negotiate another session. Be aware that the less experienced and less professional the photographer, the more likely this problem will occur. But even the best have bad days. It is your job to make clear with the photographer, before the session, what you want and expect.

The bottom line is that these headshots need to last you for a couple of years unless you significantly change your look. You have to really like them. Whatever you send out needs to be as perfect and classy as you can get.

One final point. Make sure each 8 × 10 original from the photographer has proper contrast (nothing should be too light or too dark) since the reproduction process will increase that contrast.

REPRODUCTIONS

Your quantity prints should very closely match the original. Compare sample originals and reproductions to choose a reproduction house. Ask your photographer which house he recommends. Ask actor friends whom they use and why. Look at their pictures and see what you think. (After coming this far, you don't want to end up with an inferior product.)

It's always a good idea to have your name printed on your headshot and postcards so that the client will associate your name with your face.

What about finishes? The current nationwide standard for commercial headshots is a borderless matte or pearl finish. This means the picture covers the entire 8 × 10 area.

How many reproductions should you get? It depends on your marketing strategy. If you are planning to do a mass mailing, the larger the quantity you order, the cheaper each piece. Think through your marketing plan before you order. You don't want to have more than you will use and you can always have more made.

Now let's take a look at some examples of good commercial headshots in Figure 4-1. Once you have a chance to look them over, try to determine what each actor is saying to you or what action each is playing.

Figure 4–2 shows examples of portrait shots. The smiling shots are primarily used for commercials. The more serious shots are used for legit and soap opera work.

photo by Arthur Cohen

Kevin Fennessy

photo by Linda Holt

Sue Nichols

Figure 4–1 Headshots

photo by Joe Henson

Ellen Colton

photo by Lynn Wayne

DeMorge L. Brown

Figure 4–1 Headshots, continued

photo by Linda Holt

Ceoria M. Coates

photo by Tom Bloom

Bob Owczarek

Figure 4–1 Headshots, continued

photo by Lynn McCann

Cheryl McMahon

photo by Lynn McCann

Ducan Putney
Figure 4–1 Headshots, continued

photo by Jim Redding

Wiley Moore

photo by Lynn McCann

Norma Fine

Figure 4–1 Headshots, continued

photo by Linda Holt

Marianne Maguire

ERIK PARILLO

photo by Lynn McCann

Erik Parillo
Figure 4–1 Headshots, continued

photo Lorin Klaris

Janis Dardaris

photo Bill Miles

Ronda Pierson
Figure 4–2 Portrait Shots

Craig Alan Edwards

photo by Ron Rinaldi

Craig Alan Edwards

Dossy Peabody

photo by Tom Bloom

Dossy Peabody

Figure 4–2 Portrait Shots, continued

Harriet Rogers

Figure 4–3 Composite Shot

You will also notice the different kinds of borders. They show the photographer's particular style. The choice is yours. Be sure to mention your choice *before* shooting begins.

Figure 4–3 is a composite shot. It is used primarily by character and older actors to show their range of types and looks. Print models often use composites for their work. When I started in the business, composite shots were the norm for on-camera work in my market. Styles come and go. It's important to keep up with the changes in your market.

Postcards

Postcards, with a single picture or with two contrasting shots, like one commercial and one legit, are an excellent way to keep in touch with your clients. Which pictures you use depends on the kinds of jobs you're pursuing. If you use the two-picture postcard, the most important element is that you have two truly different looks. What does this mean? It means you should have a different expression (different actions or intentions), different clothing, and different hair.

Look at the two examples in Figure 4–4.

Kevin's postcard has both his commercial and his legit shots. Notice the different clothing, hair, and expressions. They are very different, yet both are clearly Kevin.

M. LYNDA ROBINSON

Service Number AEA-SAG-AFTRA

photo by Ron Rinaldi

M. Lynda Robinson

Kevin Fennessy
AEA/AFTRA/SAG Telephone

photo by ArthurCohen

Kevin Fennessy

Figure 4–4 Postcards

Lynda's off-the-shoulder look is for soaps and film. The other is a more casual one she uses for both theatre and commercials.

Whether you choose the single or two-picture format, postcards are an important self-marketing tool.

Your Résumé

Your résumé and your headshot make up your "business card." The résumé must look as classy and professional as your picture. Some people get a terrific headshot and then fall down on the job of designing their résumé; some do the reverse. *This headshot/résumé package has to be your unique, powerful, classy masterpiece. Don't settle for less.* Together, your headshot and résumé establish the first impression a casting director or agent has of you.

GUIDELINES

Here are important guidelines for your résumé. It should:

- Be laid out in a visually pleasing format.
- Be easy to *scan*—no one *reads* résumés.
- Clearly list your name and contact phone numbers.
- Have clearly defined headings.
- List your most important credits at the top.
- Be 8 × 10 inches, and be attached to your picture.
- Look typeset.
- Have an easy-to-read typeface.
- Be printed on high-quality paper.
- List no dates. (You can list dates of college graduation if you like.)

Most producers and directors, when in an audition situation, do not have the time to actually read a résumé. So the format and content have to be designed to facilitate picking out all the critical information in a matter of seconds, ten to fifteen to be exact. Put yourself in the shoes of the director or producer. *Your résumé should pique the director's curiosity, not give him the complete story of your life.* Less is often more. The impressive highlights leave room for conversation.

"But I haven't done that much since college," you say. "I'd better add my high school plays." Are you one of those actors who are just starting out and tend to put too much on their résumés because they're trying to make up for lack of experience? Rest easy. I have seen very impressive résumés from people just starting out who made the most of their little experience in a really classy format. They made it look distinct and professional and did not apologize for it. And it looked great.

I have also seen résumés of very experienced people who listed nearly everything they'd ever done. It's overwhelming. The director doesn't know what to look at. There's just too much information.

Here is a very important rule: *do not lie on your résumé.* "So I see you can roller-skate." Gulp! Believe it or not, even in Los Angeles and New York, you run into a lot of the same people on a regular basis at auditions and jobs. It's really a pretty small world. If you lie, you won't be able to keep track of it. And you can't pretend to roller-skate. You don't want to put energy into covering your lies, so just don't do it. We all start at the beginning, with no experience. It's no secret, and nothing to be ashamed of. Make your credits look great, but don't lie or apologize.

Here are a few more guidelines worth noting:

- Among the *phone numbers,* list your agent's. If you don't have an agent, list your service or voice mail number. In smaller markets, actors list their home phone numbers and use an answering machine.
- *Addresses* are usually not listed. Actors in smaller markets often do list them. (They feel safe doing so.)
- *Social security numbers* may be listed in larger markets at the request of your agent. They are not listed in smaller markets. (With a name, social security number, date of birth, and address, or any combination, a scam artist could really do a number on you. You decide which items you want listed. The fewer the better in the larger markets. You can provide this information for a job when asked. Not printing this information on your résumé will not keep you from getting a job. Remember, résumés can end up *anywhere.*)
- If you have a *fax machine,* list it. However, you do not need a fax machine to get work.
- Always list your *union affiliations* at the top.
- If you are an expert at using an *ear prompter,* list it. Ear prompters are rarely, if ever, used in commercials.

By way of explanation, ear prompters are typically used by spokespeople and narrators in corporate videos, where the narrator is talking directly to the camera. They are used by actors for live presentations, such as trade shows, since memorizing very long scripts in a few days is extremely difficult. They can also be used in place of a teleprompter. An ear prompter consists of a microcassette recorder, a neck loop, and an earpiece similar to a hearing aid. The neck loop acts as a transmitter, which allows you to hear, through your earpiece, what you have recorded on your cassette recorder. You must have excellent ear prompter skills in order to use it professionally.

Finally, modeling credits are a no-no on an acting résumé. The theory is that anyone can model but not everyone can act.

THEATRE CREDITS

Even though you may be pursing on-camera work, casting directors and agents want to know that you are a "trained" actor. Be sure to list your theatre credits.

Should I List the Commercials I've Done?

Do not list commercials in which you have played a principal role. Why? If you have made a commercial for Toyota and you are currently auditioning for Ford, it makes clients uncomfortable to know that you did a spot for Toyota. They might worry that your face will still be associated with Toyota. However, if directly asked, you should tell the truth. If it has been a year or two since the Toyota spot quit airing, you can report that.

In the case of two competing companies, the client is protected by an exclusivity clause. It states that "if you are a union member and are currently appearing as an on-camera principal in a commercial for one company, you are not allowed to appear as an on-camera principal in a commercial for a competing company at the same time." This is a union rule and must be honored. This also applies if the commercial is not currently airing but you are being paid for it while it is "on hold" for possible later airing. Violation of this clause is very serious and can cost you work, money, and reputation.

So if you don't list the actual commercial clients, what do you list? You can say, "On-camera principal for national and regional spots." Or you can list the number of commercials you've done (if it is substantial), such as "50 national and regional spots." If you have a demo tape of your commercials, you can say "tape available upon request," "audio (if you do voice-overs) and video tapes available," or "demo reel on request." If you don't have any commercial credits yet, so be it. Leave out the category.

Special Skills

The special skills category is very useful for casting directors and agents since they are often asked to find actors who can do "special" things. By listing your special skills you make the casting director's job a little easier. However, the skills must be *special*—skills you can perform proficiently, such as horseback riding, driving a motorcycle, ice- or roller-skating, playing the piano, hang gliding, playing baseball or hockey. Typing or using a computer is not a special skill because anyone can *look* proficient when doing them on-camera. You get the picture. You have to be able to look as if you can do it well on-camera if you list it.

I hope you are not one of those actors who put hang gliding on your résumé and believe you can learn it overnight, after you've been cast! Director Danny Driscoll says there is nothing quite so upsetting as an actor who lies about a special skill that is vital to the shooting of a commercial. This kind of lie can cost the production time and money and seriously damage your career.

Other important "special skills" include languages you speak fluently (if you're not fluent, specify your level of proficiency). In the larger markets, a casting director can always find someone who is fluent in just about any language, so don't fudge this credit or any of them for that matter. Dialects and impersonations are important to include, as well as any sports you play well.

Try to make the special skills and training sections of your résumé an added bonus rather than the largest part. If you're just starting out, it may be difficult, but work towards finding a balanced format.

Finally, remember that your résumé is an evolving piece of art, which must be updated regularly.

Some examples of résumés are shown in Figure 4–5. They all have some excellent and effective qualities. Borrow the good aspects from each of them to put together your perfect résumé.

Your Working Wardrobe

What should you have in your working wardrobe? Again, look to TV to see what people are wearing in commercials. As a rule of thumb, classic and conservative is best. Remember, the camera does not like loud colors, big prints, certain small-check patterns, sharply contrasting or thin stripes. Pick clothing that is representative of your type: a young mom, a college student, a doctor, or a blue-collar type. Your clothing should fit well. Once you have two or three basic outfits in each of your types, you can mix and match.

Demo Reels

The need for a professional demo reel varies from market to market and time to time. Ten years ago all the CDs wanted them. Then, six or seven years passed when few people wanted them. Now we're back to the time when it is a necessity to have one again.

The most critical point is this: a demo reel must be a sampling of principal work you've done professionally. It should be no more than four minutes in length. You need several excellent clips on your reel. If you are a newcomer, wait until you have professional credits before putting one together.

Producing a professional reel is time-consuming and costly. Be prepared to spend time and money. Find a good production house that has a history with actors' demo reels. For a detailed discussion of the process, see an article called "The Video Demo: Making the Rounds on Tape," from the June 25, 1993 issue of *Back Stage,* the performing arts weekly out of New York.

At the same time you're developing and improving your physical tools, you can be working on improving your commercial techniques. Let's get started with analyzing the copy.

J. Michael Bloom and Associates

TALENT AGENCY

TOM KEMP
AEA SAG AFTRA

FILMS FOR TELEVISION

THE KENNEDYS OF MASSACHUSETTS	Arthur Hill	ABC
DEADLY FORCE	Sgt. Jack Finnegan	Telecom for CBS
PAROLE	Frank	RSO for CBS
SEE HOW SHE RUNS	Norman	CLN for CBS

TELEVISION

LAW AND ORDER "In Memory of"	Heller	Universal for NBC
RACHEL'S DINNER	Dan Clough	Heinz Family Works for WCVB
AGAINST THE LAW	Mr. Merriweather	Fox
A MATTER OF PRINCIPAL	Chairman	WCVB Boston
SPENSER FOR HIRE	Lt. Frank Burke	Warner Bros. for ABC
ROLLING	Joe Becker	WGBH/Cable
MILLERS COURT (2 episodes)	Allen Carr	WCVB Boston
PARK STREET UNDER	J.J. Collins	WCVB Boston

FILM

PRIMARY MOTIVE	State Rep.	Bon Bon Films
MERMAIDS	Buzz	Orion

THEATRE

NIGHT RIDERS	Speed Demon	Berkshire Theatre Festival
HOPSCOTCH	Will	Cape Ann Playhouse
THE SEVENTY FIFTH	Cookie	Cape Ann Playhouse
TANIA	Che Guevara	Little Flags Theatre
FANSHEN	Chen Kuan	Little Flags Theatre
MUCH ADO ABOUT NOTHING	Borachio	Piccadilly Square
THE COLOR OF HEAT	Simon	Playwrights Platform
CIRCA 1933	Bart	Playwrights Platform

COMMERCIALS

Numerous national commercials, list of conflicts available upon request.

233 Park Avenue South, Floor 10, New York, NY 10003/ Telephone
9200 Sunset Blvd., Suite 710, L.A., CA. 90069/Telephone

Tom Kemp
Figure 4–5 Résumés

Deborah Hopper

SAG/AFTRA

Telephone

Hair: Red
Eyes: Green
Height: 5' 7"
Size: 8

TELEVISION

Fox Television Network
Against The Law   Principal

Westinghouse Broadcasting
Time To Care   Principal/Narrator

ABC-TV
Family Works   Co-Star

ON-CAMERA SPOKESPERSON

Polaroid
Federal Express
Sheraton Corporation
Blue Cross/Blue Shield
Digital Equipment Corporation

PRINT ADVERTISING

Magazine
Sports Illustrated
Calendar
Dunkin' Donuts
Billboard
Eye World

TRAINING

International Film Workshops:
Acting Techniques for Directors - Barry Primus
Casting for Film & TV - Jane Alderman, C.S.A.

Film Industry Workshops:
Dave Madden's Voice-Over Lab
Tom Williams' Animation Voice-Over Lab

FEATURE FILM

The Verdict   Nurse/under 5
Sidney Lumet, director

Mermaids   Emily Bronte/under 5
Richard Benjamin, director

Witches of Eastwick   Nurse/under 5
George Miller, director

The Bostonians   Ms. Coffin/under 5
James Ivory, director

VOICE-OVER & NARRATION

National Public Radio
Humor Segments
International Museum Exhibit:
Earth Over Time
Japanese Language Project for
Harvard University
Audio Annual

STAGE

Crimes of the Heart
Lead: Meg Magrath

SPECIAL SKILLS

Lead Vocalist: *Alto*
Cartoon/Animation Voices
Dialects: *Authentic*
Southern, New England,
Mid-Western, British, Irish, Brooklyn
Musical Comedy writer/performer
On–Camera Commercials Instructor
Audio Prompter Expert

Voice & video tapes and commercial credits available upon request.

Deborah Hopper

Figure 4–5 Résumés, continued

Janis Dardaris

SAG - AFTRA - AEA

Service

FILM & TELEVISION

LAW & ORDER	Florence Mackey	NBC
MY LITTLE GIRL	Florence	Merchant Ivory Productions
	(Geraldine Page's niece)	
SOUNDING	Karen *(lead)*	Joel Coen
TEEN FATHER *(w/ Corey Parker)*	Angela *(principal)*	ABC After School Special
THE UNDEFEATED RHUMBA CHAMP	Nurse Harris *(lead)*	PBS
GEORGE WASHINGTON	Millie *(barmaid)*	ABC mini-series
TREASUREQUEST III	Casey Faison *(lead)*	PBS

N.Y. THEATRE

BREAKING LEGS	Angie	Promenade Theatre
(w/ Philip Bosco & Vincent Gardenia)		
MATT THE KILLER	Ann (lead)	Playwright's Horizons
FINDING DONIS ANNE	Rachel	Westbeth Theatre Center
ORGASMO ADULTO ESCAPES	one-woman show	" "
FROM THE ZOO		
THE GREEN DEATH	Oceana Pacifica	Actors' Outlet
THE ADMIRABLE CRICHTON	Eliza (Tweeny)	Spectrum Theatre Rep.

• Circle Rep., former company member

REGIONAL

THE APPLICANT / ONE FOR THE ROAD	Ms. Piffs/Gila	Walnut Street Theatre
WAITING FOR THE PARADE	Catherine	" "
OTHELLO	Desdemona	" "
MACBETH	Lady Macbeth	" "
A MIDSUMMER NIGHT'S DREAM	Titania	" "
SHOULDERS	Linda	Philadelphia Drama Guild
AS IS	Lily/Ensemble	The Philadelphia Company
TOP OF THE WORLD	Katherine	Philadelphia Festival Theatre
TALKING WITH...	Audition	The People's Light & Theatre Co.
A DAY IN THE DEATH OF JOE EGG	Sheila	*(Acting Company Member)*
ARMS AND THE MAN	Louka	" "
A LOVELY SUNDAY FOR CREVE COEUR	Helena	" "
MRS. CALIFORNIA	Babs	" "
JULIUS CAESAR	Portia	" "
THE CRUCIBLE *(w/ George Hearn)*	Susanna Walcott	Bucks County Playhouse
THE LADY'S NOT FOR BURNING	Jennet Jourdemayne	Hedgerow Theatre
AS YOU LIKE IT	Rosalind	Three Rivers Shakespeare
RICHARD II	Duchess of York	" "
TWELFTH NIGHT	Olivia	Contemporary Shakespeare
HENRY V	Katherine	" "
TROILUS & CRESSIDA	Helen	" "
OTHELLO	Emilia	" "
HAMLET	Gertrude	" "
CANDIDA	Candida	" "

SKILLS

Improvisational Comedy, Sing (Soprano), Basic Ballet, Jazz & Tap, Character Voices, All Dialects,
Can Type, Drive Stick-shift, Very Athletic, Horseback Riding, Rollerskating, Swim

Janis Dardaris

Figure 4–5 Résumés, continued

Christopher Flockton

AEA SAG AFTRA

Height:	6'0"	Eyes:	Blue
Weight:	175 lbs	Hair:	Light Brown
S.S.#:		Voice:	Baritone

Theatre

And a Nightingale Sang	Norman	Porthouse Theatre Company, OH
The Philanderer	Charteris	Lyric Stage Company, MA
A Christmas Carol	Scrooge/Cratchit (understudy)	Huntington Theatre Company, MA
A Midsummer Night's Dream	Demetrius	Worcester Forum Theatre, MA
A Christmas Carol	Fred/Young Scrooge	Merrimack Repertory Theatre, MA
Henry IV Part I	Sir Walter Blunt	Palace Theatre, NH
My Fair Lady	Colonel Pickering	Palace Theatre, NH
Joe Egg	Bri	Equity Showcase, MA
Victoria Station	Cab Driver	The Studio at The Huntington Theatre, MA
Third Person	Elliott/Robin	The Studio at The Huntington Theatre, MA
The Frog Princess	Gossip the Jester	The Studio at The Huntington Theatre, MA
The Adventures of Maggie Blume	Ian Blume	The Studio at The Huntington Theatre, MA
The Second Coming	Father	Playwright's Platform, MA
DeathTrap	Sidney Bruhl	Vintage Repertory Company, ME
Wait Until Dark	Harry Roat	Vintage Repertory Company, ME
A Child's Christmas in Wales	Narrator	Vintage Repertory Company, ME
The Lion in Winter	Geoffery	Thomas Playhouse, ME
Glengarry Glen Ross	Williamson	Vokes Theatre, MA

Film/Television

Dirty Dancing	Waiter/Bellhop	Vestron Pictures
Blown Away	Police Photographer	MGM
True Lies	Security Officer	Omega Sector, Inc.
The Buccaneers	Waiter	BBC / WGBH
Unsolved Mysteries	Bar Fly	Cosgrove-Meurer Productions (NBC)
Guests of the Nation	Belcher	Boston University
The Script	Bob Armitage	Harvard University

Commercial/Industrial

Dunkin Donuts	Harvard Community Health Plan	Lockheed Corporation
Hands On Learning (Oracle)	Li'l Peach Convenience Stores	Spinnaker Software
Akari Hair Care Products	DDI Multimedia	

Training

- ➢ American Academy of Dramatic Arts (New York)
- ➢ Improvisation - Michael Allosso (Boston)
- ➢ On-Camera Acting - Pat Dougan (Boston)
- ➢ Commercial Audition Technique - Dan Driscoll (Boston)
- ➢ Private Coaching - Craig Foley S.S.D.C.(Boston)

Special Abilities

- ➢ Authentic English accent. British dialects (BBC, Cockney, Midlands, Liverpudlian, Irish, Scottish, etc.), Australian, General and Standard American, more
- ➢ Expert computer operator - both IBM and Macintosh
- ➢ Fluent in Techno-babble
- ➢ Sports: skiing (downhill, cross country, water), cricket, squash, rollerblading
- ➢ Drive standard, automatic, and motorcycle
- ➢ Belly dancing

10/24/94

Christopher Flockton

Figure 4–5 Résumés, continued

HARRY GOLD ASSOCIATES

Talent and Literary Agency

3500 WEST OLIVE AVENUE SUITE 1400
BURBANK, CALIFORNIA 91505

(818) 769-5003   FAX (818) 955-6411

DAVID MARCIANO
AFTRA/SAG

Address
Telephone
SS#

Height: 6'
Weight: 165 lbs.
Eyes: Hazel
Hair: Brown

FILM

		DIRECTOR
COME SEE THE PARADISE	Krieg	Alan Parker
HARLEM NIGHTS	Tony	Eddie Murphy
LETHAL WEAPON II	Cop	Richard Donner

TELEVISION

CIVIL WARS	10/13ths	Gregory Hoblit
BLACK JACK SAVAGE	Guest Star	Tucker Gates
MAVERICK SQUARE (PILOT 1990)	Series Reg.	ABC/Steve Miner
THREE FOR THE MONEY (PILOT 1990)	Series Reg.	NBC/Lorimar
KISS SHOT (MOW)	Lead	Jerry London
POLICE STORY (MOW)	Guest Star	ABC
STREET OF DREAMS (MOW)	Guest Star	CBS
TICKETS PLEASE (PILOT 1988)	Series Reg.	CBS
VIETNAM WAR STORY	Guest Star	Jack Sholder
CHINA BEACH	Guest Star	Rod Holcomb
DUET	Guest Star	UBU Productions
WISEGUY	Guest Star	Larry Shaw

THEATRE

EXIT 188	Taledo	Michael Fosberg
TALK TO ME LIKE THE RAIN	Man	April Webster
STREET SCENE	Cop	Richard Morof
AWAKE & SING	Schlosser	Ron Rietchel
STREAMERS	Martin/Hinson	Ted Davis
THE CRUCIBLE	Putnam	Will Huddleston
THE WATER ENGINE	Morton Gross	Ingrid Sonnichsen
MOTHER COURAGE	Sergeant	Mort Kaplan
SHE STOOPS TO CONQUER	Diggory	Hope A. Willis
THE MACHINE STOPS	Blind Man	Paul Warner

Northeastern University: B.S., College of Arts & Sciences
Drama Studio of London at Berkeley: MFA Equivalent
Gordon Hunt: Scene Study, Los Angeles

David Marciano
Figure 4–5 Résumés, continued

Christopher Dawson — Telephone

Non-Union	Height: 5'10"	Eyes: Blue-Green Hair: Brown
(Eligible performer AEA)	Weight: 155	Voice-Over Demo Tape Available

Corporate Video

Merck Pharmaceuticals	Paul	Shaw/Beauregard Productions
A&P Supermarkets	Robbie	Creative Video Design & Production
Flex-Rite Lumbar Support	voice-over	Carlisle Sound Studio
Volkswagon	extra	Cramer Productions

Commercials

Frank's Steakhouse/		
Rosie's Restaurant	Man with 2 dates	Cable Advertising
Cellular One (radio)	Fisherman	Mullen Advertising
Chevy Geo	extra	Cramer Productions
A&E Network	extra	Sean Tracey Associates
Shoes Here	extra	Cable Advertising
Fall Image Campaign	extra	WCVB-TV, Channel 5

Film & TV

Crazy for You scene		
(Alan Myerson, director)	Brian	The Int'l Film & Television Workshops
Oatmeal	Mark	Boston University
Stop the Music video	Leading Man	BTL Inc.
Against the Law	extra	Lemon Sky Productions
From the Hip	extra	De Laurentiis Entertainment Group

Recent Theater

The Lisbon Traviata	Paul	New Repertory Theatre
Fallen Angels	Fred	Back Alley Theater
The Man Who Came to Dinner	Sandy	Lyric Stage
The Little Foxes	Leo (understudy)	Huntington Theatre Company
Another Country	Fowler	Triangle Theater Company

Special Skills

Dialects/character voices, singing range: bass-baritone, bartending, free-weights/nautilus, carpentry, roller skating, swimming, visual art, basketball, operating heavy farm equipment.

Christopher Dawson

Figure 4–5 Résumés, continued

MERLE PERKINS
AEA / SAG / AGVA

actress/singer

Telephone

Height: 5'10"

Weight: 135

Eyes, Hair: Dk. Brown

THEATRE

LIVING IN EXILE	*The Vocalist*	Merrimack Repertory Co.
COLE	*Player*	Lyric Stage Company
JESUS CHRIST SUPERSTAR	*Simon Zealots*	American Stage Festival
JACQUES BREL	*Player*	Broadway On Tour, Ltd.
CHARLOTTE'S WEB	*Charlotte*	Wheelock Family Theatre
A PARTY OF ONE	*Player*	Theatre Lobby
ESTHER	*Narrator*	The Jewish Theatre of New England
ESTHER	*Narrator*	European Tour /Living Arts
OPENING DOORS	*Mothers*	Performers Ensemble
THE SOUND OF MUSIC	*Maria*	Wheelock Family Theatre
HAIR	*Dionne*	Manchester Palace Theatre
PEACE/ MNP SOVIET UNION TOUR	*Actor/Co-Director*	Children Are The Future
OLIVER	*Nancy*	Wheelock Family Theatre
TINTYPES	*Susannah*	Nickerson Theatre
THE KING AND I	*Lady Thiang*	Wheelock Family Theatre
HARLEM RENAISSANCE	*Bessie Smith*	Boston Arts Group
WORKING	*Maggie Holmes*	Michael Allosso
ARE YOU READY MY SISTER?	*Harriet Tubman*	Underground Railway Theatre

FILM AND VIDEO

MERMAIDS (FEATURE FILM)	*Nurse Garnell*	Orion Pictures/Axium Enterprises
AMERICA'S MOST WANTED	*Laidella OBrien*	Fox Network
AGAINST THE LAW	*Lawyer*	Fox Network/Lemon Sky Pro.
SEXUAL HARASSMENT	*Victim*	New England Telephone
SHERATON HOTELS	*Hotel Manager*	Multivision
EVERYTHING'S FINE	*Work-aholic Mother*	Blue Cross/Blue Shield
SONESTA HOTEL	*Singing Hotel Manager*	McGuire & Downes, Inc.
JORDAN MARSH	*Working Professional, mother*	Videocraft
USSR TOUR 1987 [DOCUMENTARY FILM]		Children Are The Future

TRAINING AND TEACHING EXPERIENCE

Boston University	Bachelor of Music	1985
	Tanglewood Institute: Outstanding Singer Award	1980
	Theatre Institute Assistant Teaching Fellow	1982-1984

Walnut Hill School of Performing Arts - Teacher of Musical Theatre	1983-1984
Wheelock College - Young Artists' Program Teacher of Musical Theatre	1989-present

SKILLS

Dance - Jazz, Modern	Juggling	Dialects	American Sign Language

Merle Perkins

Figure 4–5 Résumés, continued

NATALIE ROSE (E.M.C.)

Telephone

HT:5' 7"/WT: 125 lbs.
EYES: Brown
HAIR: Auburn

THEATRE

My Mother Said I Never Should		**Margaret** (US)
	Huntington Theatre Company- dir: Charles Towers	
The Way of the World		**Marwood**(US)/**Peg** (US - on 2x)
	Huntington Theatre Company- dir: Sharon Ott	
Educating Rita		**Rita**
	Thomas Playhouse, ME. - dir: Kimberly Faris	
The Lion in Winter		**Alais**
	Thomas Playhouse, ME. - dir: Melissa Wentworth	
The Crucible		**Elizabeth Proctor**
	Brandeis University; Spingold Theater - dir: Evan Yionoulis	
Mad Forest		**Angel, Doctor, etc./ Translator**
	Brandeis University; Laurie Theater - dir: Judy Braha	
Three Sisters		**Irina**
	Brandeis University; Laurie Theater - dir: Theodore Kazanoff	
As You Like It		**Phebe**
	Brandeis University; Laurie Theater - dir: Daniel Gidron	
A Chorus of Disapproval		**Rebecca Huntley-Pike**
	Brandeis University; Laurie Theater - dir: Daniel Gidron	
Landscape of the Body		**Joanne**
	Brandeis University; Merrick Theater - dir: Lee Thompson	
Waiting for Lefty		**Florrie**
	Brandeis University; Laurie Theater - dir: Theodore Kazanoff	
Strangers on Earth		**Priscilla**
	New Boston Rep Theater - dir: Kent Paul	
Richard III		**Duke of York**
	Open Door Theater - dir: Larry Blamire	
The Almighty Lottery		**Connie**
	Brandeis University; Laurie Theater - dir: Jess Lynn	
Talking With...		**French Fries**
	Back Alley Theater - dir: Helen Wheelock	

FILM/VIDEO

"Captiva" segment: Polaroid Industrial	Koplow & Stark Creative, inc.	Principal
Law firm industrial: Sexual Harassment		Principal
Showcase Cinema Promotional	Videocraft Productions	Extra

EDUCATION

MFA Brandeis University: May 1993
    ACTING: Theodore Kazanoff, Evan Yionoulis
    ON-CAMERA ACTING : Pat Dougan
    VOICE/SPEECH: Mary Lowry, Alex Davis
    MOVEMENT: Susan Dibble, Annie Loui, Erika Batdorf
    COMBAT: Robert Walsh
SKILLS: Dialects, SAFD certified actor/combatant, cycling , speak French,

Natalie Rose

Figure 4–5 Résumés, continued

Analyzing the Copy and Finding the Key Message

5

*I*n 1976, when I did my first acting in commercials, they were consistently thirty to sixty seconds long. The messages were "word"-oriented, and actors were delivering more direct sales pitches than they do today. Over the last few years, because it has become more expensive to buy airtime, and since ad budgets have been shrinking, copywriters have had to make more creative use of smaller time slots. Many of today's commercials are ten to fifteen seconds in length, dominated by visual images and technical sophistication. There are fewer on-camera actors, and more product images with voice-overs. Today's TV commercials are aimed less at our conscious, verbal side and more at our intuitive side, with lots of quick images. The result is that commercials must grab our attention while leaving us with a clear, single message. Dan Driscoll, owner and director at September Productions in Boston, wisely points out that a commercial should leave you with a single thought or message. Our goal, then, is to identify that single key message in each kind of commercial.

Why is this important? When you understand the key message, you can hit the key words, and make strong, interesting transitions by playing clear actions; in this way you increase your chances of winning the job. Remember, you will be competing with five to one hundred or more actors for each job, depending on your market. Having the right "look" is important, too. But understanding the key message—and demonstrating that understanding—is critical.

The Storyboard

As a first step to understanding any commercial, study the storyboard. *The storyboard is your bible.* A storyboard is an artist's hand-drawn pictures of the action of the commercial, shot by shot. The storyboard provides valuable information. It shows you what the creative team wants to achieve with the commercial, and what it will look like when it's shot. It tells you the story, who your character is, what she looks like, her relationships in the story, what actions she takes, and what she says or the announcer says—very important. Figure 5–1 is an excellent example of a storyboard. Study it. (A larger version of this storyboard is on page 176.)

Storyboards are drawn for all three major kinds of on-camera commercials today involving actors: the "spokesperson," "slice-of-life," and "quick-cuts." Let's define each and look for the key messages.

Kinds of Commercials

Spokesperson

As a spokesperson, you are talking directly to the camera about the product. There is a wide range of spokesperson commercials, from "soft sell" to "hard sell." A hard sell example is the car dealer ad, where the spokesperson is upbeat, excited, bigger than life, encouraging you to "come down and buy now!" Examples of soft sell are the Taster's Choice and the Monistat 7 ads.

Slice-Of-Life

Slice-of-life commercials are just that, a moment of real life. You are doing something you would really do in life, such as eating in a restaurant, talking with your family, visiting your doctor, suffering from a sinus cold. You may or may not have lines. There can also be a combination of spokesperson and slice-of-life in the same commercial. An example would be an ad with a mother who is serving chicken, engrossed in dialogue with her family, while also talking directly to the camera.

Quick-Cuts

Quick-cuts are one- to five-second cameos of you as you react to a question or situation. Examples are your reaction after a bite of pizza ("Wow"), or your response to what is said about a product: "This has less sugar than the other brand" ("Really?"), or "How do you stop smoking?" ("Habitease"), or "Do you really feel this detergent is better than the others?" ("Definitely!"). Sometimes you react visually only, without any lines. Quick-cut commercials generally have several different people reacting in sequence.

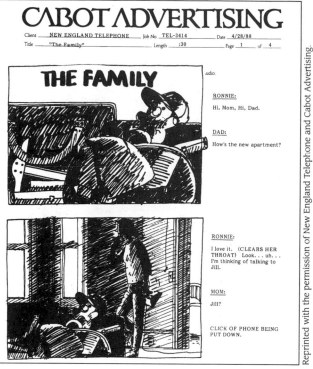

Figure 5–1, page 1

Figure 5–1, page 2

Figure 5–1, page 3

Figure 5–1, page 4

Problem-Solution-Action Message Analyses: Spokesperson

Now that you have an understanding of the three basic kinds of on-camera commercials, let's use real commercials to identify the key message in each. Let's start by using the *problem-solution-action message* method of analysis. I first learned these problem-solution analyses in a class I took at Weist-Barron. Finding the problem and solution is a common technique used in sales pitches, brochures, college papers, legal arguments, in analyzing the economy, relationships, and more. An "action message" is a spoken or unspoken directive to take action: to try it or go buy it.

With this Drake's spokesperson commercial, let's find the key message. (This commercial is reprinted with the permission of Drake's Bakeries.)

Drake's

Times are tough today, right? Prices keep going up . . . and up . . . and up. You want to hear some good news for a change? At Drake's, we're bringing our prices down. So now you get those same delicious Devil Dogs, Ring Dings, Yankee Doodles, and more . . . for less. At Drake's, all we changed was the price. And for my money, that's a change for the better.

We can best understand this copy by using the *problem-solution-action message* analysis. What is the problem? The problem is that times are tough because the price of everything keeps going up. (Times are tough today, right? Prices keep going up . . . and up . . . and up.)

The solution tells us how to solve the problem, or how this particular product solves the problem better than other products. (You want to hear some good news for a change? At Drake's, we're bringing our prices down. So now you get those same delicious Devil Dogs, Ring Dings, Yankee Doodles, and more . . . for less.) The solution to the problem is that Drake's will continue to sell you all the same great products at reduced prices.

The action message (At Drake's, all we changed was the price, and for my money, that's a change for the better) restates the solution, namely that Drake's brought the prices down, and essentially says, "Since I'm going to continue to buy Drake's products for less money, you should, too." The unwritten action message is: It cost me less, it'll cost you less, and it's still the same great product, so go out and buy it!

What is the key message? Look for repeated words. The key words "price(s)" and "change(d)" and "up" are used three times each. We know that "Prices keep going up . . ." is the problem and "bringing our prices down" is the solution to the problem. The most basic, distilled message, the single thought we're left with, is "we're bringing our prices down."

This Drake's commercial is fairly straightforward in format. The problem-solution-action message, and overall key message are not difficult to identify. But many commercials aren't nearly so clearly written and do not fit into neat analyses. Let's take a look at a slice-of-life commercial that requires a different kind of analysis to understand.

Deduction and Assumption: Analyzing a Slice-Of-Life

In the slice-of-life commercial, you are captured doing something you'd do in real life. Often you are asked to improvise at the audition, particularly if you have no lines. If you get the job, you will end up with specific lines or dialogue. Or you may be captured in action without lines as an announcer speaks over the action.

Remember to study the storyboard if it is available. But even if it isn't, it's important that you find the key message through deduction and assumption. For practice in analyzing a slice-of-life commercial without a storyboard, let's use an example from my own work. I was called in to audition for the role of a mom as part of a mom/dad couple for a bank commercial. At the first audition, there was a storyboard, but it was "in development" and had changed significantly just before the audition. (This isn't terribly unusual.) The casting director told us to ignore the storyboard. She described the commercial:

> Mom and Dad are sending their son off to college. They're giving him a set of car keys. It should be a serious good-bye, not funny. Don't make jokes. There is no copy, no set lines. I would like you to improvise the scene. I want to see you "show" both pride and sadness. You won't have a "son" at the audition. Use the camera as the son.

The actor playing the Dad and I went off to work on this. Since the storyboard was evolving, we did not have the benefit of the announcer's voice-over to help determine the key message of the whole commercial. How did we analyze the copy? To begin with, we looked at what we knew. We reviewed the information. We had been given the direction to "show" both pride and sadness while giving our son a set of car keys as he left for college. Even though we did not know the key message of the whole commercial, we knew the message for Mom and Dad: "Show pride and sadness as you give him the keys." We are sad to see him go, but we want him to have a car when he's away at college and we're proud of him. From these details, we deduced that the key message of the whole commercial was that this bank *cares* about families. Because they care, we are able to get a car loan. Because they care, this bank will help *you* get what *you* need. Of course, we could not play "this bank cares." But having *assumed* it as the key message informed our improvisation.

This method for finding the key message was *deduction and assumption*. Based on the facts, we went through a process of reasoning and came to a logical conclusion. Finally, we verbalized the key message—very important. You may think the key message, but stating it makes it concrete.

Analyzing a "Quick-Cut"

The third kind of commercial for analysis is a quick-cut. As I mentioned earlier, in a quick-cut, you are reacting in one to five seconds, with or without lines, to a question or statement. The questions may be asked out loud, or you may have to create the person who's asking the question. Quick-cuts usually show a series of different people reacting in sequence.

There is no clear-cut formula for analyzing or understanding a quick-cut. However, again, the ultimate goal is to identify the key message. In this Suds commercial, the key thought you're left with is clear.

> Voice-over announcer: Did you know that people all over the country are switching to Suds because now the soap and bleach are in the same box?

> Series of real people: Really! (We see numerous quick-cuts of different people saying "Really!")

> What is the key message? What is the single thought you're left with? "The soap and bleach are in the same box."

If we analyze this with the problem-solution-action message method, we see that the problem is implied—too many boxes. People have to use one box for soap and another for bleach. This problem justifies the solution, "The soap and the bleach are in the same box." People are switching to Suds for the convenience of using one box. The action message is unspoken and is also assumed: If people all over the country are switching, you will want to, too. Go out and buy it!

Once you understand the key message, it will help you determine how to choose your quick-cut reactions. *Your reactions should reinforce the key message.* You can't effectively move to that next step of technique until you have identified the key message.

Summary

Identifying the key message is sometimes difficult and sometimes easy. It's like trying to find the objective in a beat of a scene or play. Sometimes it's easy, but when it gets difficult, ask yourself: What is the single thought or message that the copywriter is trying to get across in the entire commercial? Use these guidelines:

1. Study the storyboard.
2. If unavailable, ask for the casting director to explain the commercial.
3. Can you identify the problem, solution, or action message?
4. What words or phrases are repeated two or more times?
5. If you have no lines or are asked to improvise, what message is your improvisation supposed to impart?
6. With the provided information, what can you deduce and assume the key message to be?
7. What is the single thought or message you're left with in the whole commercial?

Knowing the whole story will help you understand the key message and how your character contributes to it, whether you're reacting, having a dialogue, or are the spokesperson. The key message is often reiterated at the end of the commercial. Here's my message: you need to go through each stage of the process, step by step, to add to your understanding and improve your odds of winning the job. The good news is it will get easier the more you do it.

Exercises

There are several methods of analysis to find the key message. Let's try two different methods. For the first approach:

1. Go to the back of the book and pick a piece of copy. Choose a commercial without a storyboard.
2. Read it three or four times. Understand what it's saying.
3. Identify the key words. Which words or phrases, aside from the product name, are mentioned two times or more?
4. What is the single thought you're left with? Distill the words into a single message, one sentence or a key phrase. State, out loud, the key message, using the words of the copy.
5. Read the copy out loud, emphasizing the key words. Does it make sense?

For a different approach, try the problem-solution-action message method. Choose another piece of copy from the back of the book. Remember, the product solves the problem.

Do these exercises before you move on to Chapter 6. If you're in doubt about your choices, get a friend or family member involved. Have some fun with it.

Defining the Role and Developing the Character

6

Kinds of Roles

*I*n the last chapter we discussed the three major kinds of commercials being made today: spokesperson, slice-of-life, and quick-cuts. Now let's look at the variety of roles you may be asked to perform, depending on your type. Many casting decisions are made on the basis of "look" or "type." A more skillful actor might lose the job to someone with a better look for the part. The types of roles you are called in for depend largely on your look and age, assuming you have the necessary acting skills. The more you can diversify your look and skills, the wider the range of roles you may be considered for. Since there is an abundance of different types, actors tend to be typecast in larger markets more than in smaller markets.

SPOKESPERSON

The *spokesperson* is the representative for the product. As the authority on the product, her goal is to make you believe in its merits as much as she does. The spokesperson can be anyone: the owner of the company, a serious doctor talking about hemorrhoids, a casually dressed professional selling real estate, or a blue-collar worker selling mufflers. The spokesperson talks directly to camera and has arrived at this total belief in the product from personal experience. The key is to speak as the authority, with total conviction and sincerity.

SLICE-OF-LIFE AND QUICK-CUT ROLES

Slice-of-life commercials tell a story about how the product changed people's lives for the better: made them sexier, cured their colds, made their pets happier, gave them a cleaner house, got rid of their dandruff. In both the slice-of-life and quick-cut commercials, you could be any *real person* from life: housewife, dad or mom, young, middle-aged, or grand parent; a character type, blue-collar, ethnic, or just comedic; a white-collar businessman or businesswoman, secretary or executive, upscale or conservative; a sexy model, male or female; a student. You could be anybody.

Developing Your Character

When you are phoned for an audition, be sure to ask what character you will be playing. Ask where your character is in the commercial (home, store, car), to help you define the look (clothing and hair) and point of view. Dad at the office will look and act different from Dad at home.

Remember that in most commercials you are playing *yourself* as a young dad, student, or grandmother, with certain character qualities. Your character may represent funny, good-natured, shy, sweet, sexy, or apprehensive characteristics. As a person you have all these qualities and more. You do not have time to develop a character the way you do in plays or films. You are cast primarily because of your look or type. It is assumed you have the acting skills. So play yourself with the qualities of the character.

The copy and storyboard hold most of the answers to your character and acting choices. They tell you who you are, what you are doing, what you are saying, your point of view, whom you are talking to or interacting with, what you look like (as drawn by an ad agency artist), and what you are wearing.

However, to fully evolve your character and develop the scene, you need to know what your character *wants*. To achieve this, you play actions, a critical process for all good actors.

Choosing and Playing Actions 7

Great! You've landed a role in a commercial. The day of the shoot arrives and you report to the set for makeup and wardrobe. You know your lines. You're called to the set to rehearse. After the first rehearsal the director says, "Be more excited," or "Be funnier." Yikes! These are emotions, results. As any good actor knows, you can't play results. Actors try to do it all the time, but it doesn't work. It's not convincing. I don't believe it. Robert L. Benedetti writes, "Acting is *doing* things that need to be done. Acting is *not* 'being a character' or 'creating an emotion.' Emotion is a by-product of action" (*The Actor At Work*, Prentice-Hall, 1986). Playing an emotion or result doesn't make any connection with the person you're talking to. If you are not actively connecting with that character in the scene or lens, you won't be believable to anyone. What do you do?

Unlike rehearsing for a play, where there is time for process, commercials are oriented toward "immediate results." Why? Because time is money. The client has hired the ad agency, which has hired the production company and you to deliver the finished product in the shortest time possible. It costs a fortune to make a commercial, and you have to be prepared to offer as many different reads as many times as required. *And you are often directed to play an emotion—a result.*

The Action Or "I Want To . . ."

How do you give the client and director what they want without playing a result? You play an action, what I call "I want to. . . ." You actively try to get something from or do something to the other character, whether that character is a real person in the scene or that imaginary friend in the lens. You don't play "I'm angry" or "I'm excited." You play an active need, an "I want to . . ."—"I want to excite you," or "I want to make you feel better," or "I want to tease you." We see you in pursuit, trying to get something from the character you're talking to, which gives the director the "result" he's looking for. Your choice is exciting, alive, and believable, not fixed or phony. Each time you choose an action, make a personal commitment to achieve it.

If you have training in the theatre, you know this technique is the same as choosing an objective and then playing actions to achieve it. I like to call it "I want to . . ." because it gives me a more immediate visual image of what I'm trying to get from the other actor. And it works!

How Many "I Want to . . ."s Should I Choose?

Choose a different "I want to . . ." for each major subject change. Since the copywriter has to get a number of specific points across in each commercial, the subject changes a few times from beginning to end, sometimes subtly, sometimes rather directly. For example, in our Drake's commercial, the beginning section talks about how times are tough. The next section tells us Drake's is lowering its prices. At the end, the subject is changed again to point out that all of this is a direct financial benefit to me (Drake's spokesperson) and you (the viewer). So the subject has changed at least three times. I can choose a different action for each to provide contrast for the commercial.

Let's choose an action to play or an "I want to . . ." for each of those changes. I want *to empathize* with you: "Times are tough today, right? Prices keep going up . . . and up . . . and up." I want *to entice* you: "You want to hear some good news for a change?" There could be another change here. I want *to excite* you: "At Drake's we're bringing our prices down. So now you get those same delicious Devil Dogs, Ring Dings, Yankee Doodles, and more . . . ." Another change—I want *to surprise* you: "For less." Another change—I want *to assure* you that the quality is as good as ever: "At Drake's, all we changed was the price." And finally, I want *to convince* you beyond a doubt: "And for my money, that's a change for the better." So in a thirty-second commercial, we've found seven different active "I want to . . ."s to play. This will provide plenty of contrast while keeping the commercial flowing.

At first, you may find that the choices you make are flabby, not strong. Or they may not really be playable or active. For example, choosing "I want to tell you" is much less active than "I want to excite you." "Tell" is more passive.

This technique requires thought and patience. It requires practice. Start small. Try for three "I want to . . ."s at first. Attach an "I want to . . ." to each major subject change in the commercial.

CREATE A LIST

Make sure your choices add to the message of the commercial. Study the storyboard and make sure your choices reflect the intent of your character in the commercial. Actions should be:

- simple.
- strong.
- active verbs.
- playable.
- positive.
- specific.

The best actions are directed to another person and depend on that person's response, even if you have to create the response of an imaginary person in the camera. Let's list some "I want to . . ."s, or actions.

I want to challenge you.	I want to tease you.
I want to quiz you.	I want to convince you beyond a
I want to entice you.	doubt.
I want to grab you.	I want to thrill you.
I want to embarrass you.	I want to share this secret with you.
I want to surprise you.	I want to make you curious.
I want to make you feel better.	I want to excite you.
I want to cheer you up.	I want to encourage you.
I want to justify my position.	I want to reassure you.
I want to charm you.	I want to dazzle you.
I want to compliment you.	I want to win you over.

The list could be endless, as long as you can actually *play* it—as long as you're actively trying to tease, excite, or surprise the person you're talking to.

In some commercials, your actions will be physical only, such as blowing your nose, typing, hammering a nail, or dialing the phone, and will involve no one but you. In these situations, it is important that you develop the whole scene so your action has context and meaning.

Exercise

Have you ever watched TV commercials with the sound off? It's instructive. Try it. Watch commercials with the sound off. Try to name the actions the actors are playing, whether a physical action, such as putting on a shirt or lifting a child, or a psychological action such as comforting a sick patient or convincing a customer to buy this Ford. Write down the actions to add to your list.

Watching television with the sound off will help you see why some actions are more effective than others. Doing this helps you see the range of actions that are possible and strengthens your own choices.

THE IMPORTANCE OF REACTING

When you do not have the benefit of playing opposite a real person in the scene and your action is directed to the camera, you must create the other character's response to your action, which causes you to react and change your action. You are doing the work for both characters, you and the one in the lens.

If you're talking to another character in a slice-of-life commercial, you will be able to see how your "I want to . . ." is affecting him, and then you can react accordingly. You won't have to create his reaction as you do when talking to the camera.

In quick-cuts you are *reacting* to a statement or question rather than initiating the action. To understand this, let's review the Suds commercial.

> Voice-over announcer: Did you know that people all over the country are switching to Suds because now the soap and bleach are in the same box?

Then we see numerous "quick-cuts" of people saying, "Really?"

Depending on what the storyboard shows you, you could be at home in your laundry room pouring an inferior detergent into your washer, in a laundromat being handed a box of Suds, or in the supermarket about to buy detergent. In each of these scenarios your reaction would be different since each scene is different. Of course, when provided, study the storyboard.

In this particular copy, we're given the benefit of being asked a specific question. So we can come up with a range of different responses to the question. We can ask the question in our minds and then react to it. Try saying in your mind, "No kidding, it's true," even though you're saying out loud, "Really!" Or in your mind, "I didn't know that," when you're saying, " Really?" Or in your mind, "Are you trying to fool me?" when out loud you're saying, "Really?" You get the idea. Think up at least three different reactions to the question that are in keeping with the storyboard and the intent of the spot.

This all sounds pretty complicated, especially since the goal of the commercial actor is to look relaxed, natural, and spontaneous. How do you do it? Well, once you acquire this technique, you will be able to do it instinctively. (Really? Really.) And even while you're learning it, once you've made your "I want to . . ." choices in preparation for an audition or a job, don't get caught up in the technique. Throw it out. Just do the commercial. Be spontaneous. The techniques will begin to stick with you. *Don't concentrate on the technique while you're doing the audition or job. Use the technique as preparation.*

MAKE STRONG, SPECIFIC CHOICES

When starting out, my students tend to skimp on choosing strong, specific "I want to . . ."s, playable, active verbs. They want to play results. And it shows. When they don't use this technique their delivery seems in limbo. It's not grounded. They "act" in the negative sense. There is little connection between the words on the page and the delivery. There is no real life in the spot, and it looks and feels superficial. When they get specific and start trying to grab, or excite, or thrill the other person, the spot comes to life. *You must truly believe what you're doing if you want the viewer to believe it.* And to believe, you cannot play a result.

Remember, it all takes time. Be patient with yourself, but practice, and use the technique. Gradually, it will stick and become second nature. Eventually, when the director says to you, "Be more excited," you will know the process required to get to that result.

Review

I've talked about starting out simply. *In the beginning, choose three "I want to . . ."s for each commercial.* When do you make the "I want to . . ." changes? When the subject changes. Try choosing an "I want to . . ." before you begin speaking for the first time, before the second major subject change, and before the third major subject change.

As we've seen with the Drake's commercial, you can choose seven or more "I want to . . ."s. Initially, however, keep it simple by choosing only three in those places where the subject changes.

Exercise

1. Go to the back of the book and choose a commercial.
2. Go through the processes of identifying the key message and defining your character.
3. Identify the three major subject changes.
4. Now choose three active "I want to . . ."s. Make sure they enhance the message of the commercial. Make them strong. And make sure each of them is clearly different, to provide contrast. Do your choices facilitate the subject changes?

5. Go to your mirror or use your camcorder and try it. Are they positive, strong, playable choices? Do they need to be more active?
6. Refine them, and try it again, until you believe what you're doing.

Remember, the most essential process in your acting technique is choosing and playing strong actions. Playing actions is the essence of good acting. I choose my actions after I have identified the key message, and in conjunction with developing my character, the relationships, and the whole scene. Knowing who you are and what you're doing in the spot naturally leads you toward choosing and playing actions. Playing strong actions must always be present in your mind and the ultimate goal of your work.

Developing the Whole Scene | 8

N ow you understand the key message, know what character you're playing, and understand how to choose and
play actions. The next step is to *discover the given circumstances and fill in the details that aren't provided in
order to develop the whole scene.* Many of the answers will be in the
copy and storyboard. Missing information—context, motives, relationships—will be yours to discover or create.

Let's explore the elements of developing the whole scene.

Basic Elements

WHOM ARE YOU TALKING TO?

Are you talking directly to the camera, or are you captured by the
camera as you talk to (1) another character or (2) an imaginary
character in the scene? Be specific about your relationship with
the person. If talking to an imaginary person or the camera, talk to
that *one* person, not the general public. Pick a good friend, parent,
spouse, child, someone that you, the actor, really know and like.
This helps make your work conversational and personable. If the
copy specifically indicates that you are talking to a stranger—for
instance, when you are stopped and asked a question by a
reporter on the street—be clear about your relationship with that
person and talk to her only, one person.

DEVELOPING RELATIONSHIPS

Once you know your relationship with the other characters in the scene—wife, child, friend—fill in the blanks within the context of the commercial. How long have you known each other? If you're shopping, is this the first or tenth time you've done it together in this spot? How do you feel about him? Body language is a great asset in establishing your relationships with other characters. If the person is your spouse or child, you can be more physical than if the person is your boss. If you are newly wed, there is bound to be some physical contact to establish this fact. How you sit and stand suggests how you feel.

Utilize the natural personalities of the actors you are working with to develop the relationships of the characters. Remember, you are using your own traits for the character. If you are a jolly person, use it. If your partner is withdrawn, use it.

DEVELOPING IMAGINARY CHARACTERS

When you do not have the benefit of a "live" person in the scene, you must establish that character. Suppose you are talking to your daughter in the scene but no actor is representing her. Make choices about how old she is, what she looks like, the color of her hair, and, most important, how she reacts to what you are saying or doing, and where she is at all times in the scene.

If you are standing talking to her, where is her eye line? Have you established her as a nine-year-old, for example? Does she move around during the scene? Make any imaginary person real to you.

PHYSICALLY SET UP THE SCENE

Decide where everyone and everything is in the scene. Decide where each person is positioned in relation to you and the camera. This is an important rule whether you're working solo or with another actor. You want to be seen, and so do your fellow actors. It is best to put imaginary characters directly in the camera, or out front, just to the right or left of it, not over your right or left shoulder. Otherwise your face will be in profile.

If you need a chair or props, set it up so that you can be seen by the camera. Most audition rooms have a chair or two. You may have to mime the props—see what's available and use what you can.

Where will you begin the scene? Does it make sense to start your action off-camera and walk into frame? Or is it best to start on-camera? Do you begin the scene with the copy or in the middle of a dialogue? What happens at the end? Do you stop with the words of the copy? Do you exit the frame? What makes sense for the commercial? Make clear choices that add to the intent.

KEEP IT SIMPLE

While making specific, strong choices, keep them simple. Don't clutter the scene with too much business in an effort to show how clever you are. For example, look at the Drake's copy again. Let's say that as the spokesperson you are a teacher talking directly to your friend, another teacher. Suppose you decide that you're handing out Devil Dogs to a classroom of schoolchildren all through the spot. It will weaken your work, hence the message as well, unless you decide *when* and *how often* you hand a Devil Dog to one of the imaginary students. To keep it simple, I would hand the product to one student *before* I started talking and hand one to each of two or three students *after* I finished talking. If I handed them out during the whole commercial, it would be distracting because the viewers would be following my physical actions rather than hearing the message. These actions give the scene a beginning and an ending. Even though they are not specified in the copy, the actions add to the story.

VISUALIZE THE WHOLE SCENE

Once you've got it all defined, visualize the whole scene. Make a mental image of the scene from beginning to end. When working solo, visualize the characters and your interactions with them. Visualize your actions. Visualize the physical environment you've set up for the scene. Make everything believable to you. Visualize how you will make physical adjustments in the audition room. Then rehearse it a few times. Visualizing keeps you grounded when you have few physical elements to hang on to or no actors to work with. Remember to plan to do two or three different reads. These techniques will make your work sharp and fully developed. The auditors will be impressed with your creativity.

Developing "The Bank That Cares"

Now let's practice these techniques on real copy. Remember the improvised audition for the bank that cares on pages [52-53] of Chapter 5? As you recall, we were told:

> Mom and Dad are sending their son off to college. They're giving him a set of car keys. It should be a serious good-bye, not funny. Don't make jokes. There is no copy, no set lines. I would like you to improvise the scene. I want to see you "show" both pride and sadness. You won't have a "son" at the audition. Use the camera as the son.

We determined that the key message was: this bank *cares* (about us.)

SETTING UP THE SCENE

We decided the location of the scene was in the entryway of the house. The living room was on our left, the coat closet on our right, and the stairs to the second floor behind us. The front door was open, and our son (in the camera) was about to leave for college. He was standing there with his army duffel bag. We had not yet said our final good-byes. This provided us with urgency.

It was a sunny, warm, late-August day, ten o'clock in the morning. We were planning to surprise him with the car keys, the new car. Giving him the car keys gave us an *action to play* rather than just being proud and sad. We needed to have the characteristics of pride and sadness while actively doing something.

DEVELOPING THE RELATIONSHIPS

I called our son "Billy," and sometimes "honey." I made him a blond eighteen-year-old, in jeans and a white tee shirt. He was both excited and apprehensive about going off to college, so far from home. He didn't want to say good-bye. He had a hard time looking me in the eye. He was our only child. Defining the kind of person Billy was helped me choose his reactions to me. Defining him also made him real for me. I could see him.

When I'm working with someone I have never met and we have to develop a relationship and the scene in a hurry, I suggest we go to a quiet place to discuss it and make choices. The actor playing Dad was rather shy. I am outgoing. We used these traits in developing our relationship. We decided we had been married twenty years. I called him a nickname. I put my arm around his waist. He reciprocated. This established both our comfort with each other and our sadness at seeing Billy leave. We talked to each other as well as Billy.

BEGINNING AND ENDING THE SCENE

Given the shyness and self-consciousness of the actor playing Dad, we decided to begin the scene by my pulling him into the frame and encouraging him to give Billy the car keys. We decided what prompted us into the room at that moment (Billy was leaving in ten minutes). We decided to end the scene by waving good-bye to Billy while comforting each other. We roughly rehearsed our dialogue to get across the key words (we're proud of you, we're going to miss you, call when you get there, drive safely), making sure to interact.

REVISITING EMOTIONS

To make my work as believable as possible, I took time after developing the whole scene to explore how I would feel if this were happening to me in real life. I didn't want to just put on a proud or sad "face." I needed to play actions. How would I feel losing a son? Our lives would never be the same. He would not live at home anymore. No more seeing him every day, taking care of him, sharing his concerns and hopes and laughs. Maybe I didn't really want him to go. I used the "emotion memory" that Konstantin Stanislavski talks about in *An Actor Prepares,* published by Theatre Arts Books in New York. This is an emotional recall that brings back feelings actors have previously felt in real life. I revisited my feelings when my real daughter left for college. I used these recalled feelings to make our "son" a real person, even though he wasn't at the audition, and I felt real sadness and tension.

Developing the relationships with this kind of detail and urgency helped me play two strong actions. First, I wanted to keep from crying in front of Billy. Second, I needed to pull Dad into action. Of course, the actor playing Dad had his actions, too. All this detail made our scene work.

VISUALIZING

Finally, I visualized the scene, the people, the place, and the actions. Then we rehearsed it a few times and went in to audition. Remember to transfer your visualization into the audition room, since you are in a different physical space. Do this quickly, in just a few seconds. Place the other characters in the same relationship to the camera that you placed them outside the audition room. And always picture the camera's place in the scene when you're rehearsing without a camera.

You might wonder how we involved the bank in the improvisation. We didn't. The goal of the audition was to see us in action in a real-life situation. Our analysis and development of this slice-of-life commercial went pretty well. I got the job. It ended up being a slice-of-life spot with a voice-over to tie in the key message, "This bank cares."

Preparing Different Reads

Be prepared to provide more than one interpretation, or *read*, of the commercial while playing the same character. This involves altering the qualities or point of view of the character. For example, you could be warm and friendly, or playful, or conspiratorial, if the copy gives room for these kinds of interpretation. Then, within each of these reads, you would choose at least three different "I want to . . ."s. You would not have the same "I want to . . ." or action for a "playful" read as you would for a "conspiratorial" read.

You will notice that "be playful," "be warm," are not actions. I am using them here to point out, again, that this is how you may be given directions. It is your job to turn these results into playable actions.

How do you choose three different "I want to . . ."s within each different read? Let's say you go into an audition having chosen a "warm, friendly" read integrating three different "I want to . . ." choices. The director may not give you any direction on the first take. He may want to see how you've interpreted the spot on your own. On the second take, if there is one, he may say, "Make her more playful." This is a general, subtle character change, which you make by altering your intentions or "I want to . . ."s. Since you started with the general characteristic of "warm, friendly," how can you adjust your three "I want to. . . 's" to reflect the new character trait of "playful"? "Playful" can be one aspect of "warm and friendly." You may use "I want to tease you," "I want to confuse you," and "I want to convince you" all in the same "playful" read. Just don't lose the subtleties and specificity of your work when implementing a general direction. Don't throw out your original interpretation. Adjust your existing work based on the new direction. But do make the adjustments.

Don't give exactly the same read for "playful" that you gave for "warm and friendly." There is nothing worse than to be given a direction and be unable to make the change. This is one of the biggest problems for beginners. They think they are making the change but they are not. *The bottom line is being able to implement direction immediately, within seconds, without losing all the subtleties you have built into the read.* This particular ability is the most critical skill in commercial acting. If you can't take direction, you won't get the jobs. And it's a technique that will enable you to respond to direction.

In your practice at home and in your preparation at the audition, start by choosing two different interpretations and eventually work up to three. This will help you in two ways. It will help you develop a mental library of different actions or "I want to . . ."s to have at your disposal. And it will enable you to implement directions quickly and precisely. These techniques will make your work sharp and fully developed.

Developing the Whole Scene with a Storyboard

Now let's practice these techniques on a commercial with copy and a storyboard. Study the Ocean Spray Refreshers Juice Drink storyboard in Figure 8–1.

Let's assume you have been called in to audition for this commercial. When you get to the audition, the first thing you want to do is read the copy, look at the pictures, and decide what single image or thought you're left with. What is the key message? It is that Ocean Spray Refreshers is the not-too-sweet juice drink for adults only.

You have been called in for one of the "Dad " roles, the Dad who gets caught hiding in his car drinking a Refresher. (As you can see, in this commercial, you are captured by the camera, not talking to it.) What do we know from the storyboard and copy? We know that all the parents in the commercial would do anything to keep from sharing their Refreshers with their kids. Our Dad is hiding in the back seat of his car where he can stretch out and relax while enjoying his juice. The car is in his dark garage (see the trash cans and rake). We can't tell if it's morning or night. Let's decide it's morning and Dad is trying to wake up. (The daughter probably wouldn't be up late at night.) We know the daughter is a little girl, as the copy says. Let's make her seven years old. Old enough to come looking for Dad. Old enough to try to get him to share his juice drink. (What does she look like? Visualize her. How tall is she? Decide so you can adjust your eye level accordingly.)

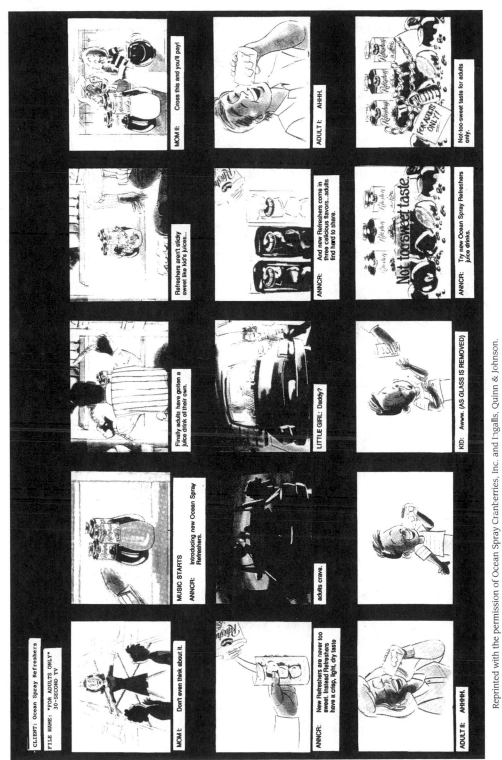

Figure 8–1 Ocean Spray Storyboard

Now let's fill in some more of the blanks that aren't provided but add to what we know about the storyboard and copy. Before the little girl finds him, Dad is quietly sitting in the car, pleased that he has some private time alone to enjoy his juice drink. (Do you want to set up the car as two chairs, side by side? Are you in the front or back seat?) He is grinning to himself, pleased that he managed to sneak out of the house unnoticed, anticipating the not-too-sweet taste of his drink. While he's pouring some Refresher from the bottle to his glass (if props are available, use them), someone suddenly throws open the left rear car door and takes him totally by surprise. (Which side are you sitting on, right or left? Which door is opened? Cheat the door forward a bit for sight lines.) There is a wide range of possible reactions. Surprised, he gasps. After his heart settles down, Dad might drink all his juice down so he won't have to share. (Action: to drink it all myself.) Or hearing his daughter lurking around before she opens the door, he might pretend he is trying to fix the radio while hiding his drink. Visualize the radio and where it is. (Action: to fool her or to hide his drink.) Or he might react by jumping out the other side of the car and trying to get away. (Action: to get away.) The possibilities are endless. And it's great to have several of these choices preplanned.

What about this choice for ending the scene? When caught by his daughter, Dad gives up and shares his Refresher with her. Why is this a poor choice? Because it is not in keeping with the key message, "the not-too-sweet juice drink for adults only." It does not add to the main theme; it is totally opposite.

Developing the Scene Without a Storyboard

To practice developing the scene without a storyboard, let's look at two examples. First, let's review our Drake's commercial.

Drake's

Times are tough today, right? Prices keep going up . . . and up . . . and up. You want to hear some good news for a change? At Drake's, we're bringing our prices down. So now you get those same delicious Devil Dogs, Ring Dings, Yankee Doodles, and more . . . for less. At Drake's, all we changed was the price. And for my money, that's a change for the better.

Since we do not have a storyboard, let's make a choice that you are a worker on the assembly line at Drake's. What time of day is it? What shift are you working? How long is the line? How many people work on it? Are you sitting or standing? How big is the building? What does your space look like? What, specifically, is your action in the production line? Boxing Ring Dings? Putting labels on boxes? Or are you in a store filling a Drake's display, or in a schoolroom handing out Drake's products to the children? Again, the important point is to make specific, strong choices that complement the copy.

For the second example, let's say you're auditioning for Clean laundry detergent. You've been told that your character is a college student in a laundromat. (What does the place look like? Where are the washers and dryers in relation to you and the camera? Are there other people there?) You're in there first thing in the morning before classes. You love the early morning. Before you begin to speak, you are smelling your towel and folding it when you're caught by surprise by your roommate (who happens to be the camera), who is holding a box of All laundry detergent. (Who is your roommate? man or woman? a good pal? hates doing the laundry?) Suppose your roommate silently asks you, since it *isn't* written in the copy, "What's so great about that detergent?" You look to the camera (your roommate), and say, "I love the smell of my clothes when I use Clean," which *is* written in the copy. (Action: I want you to smell the towel.) You do the whole spot, making strong, interesting choices for each section of the commercial. Now you've come to the end of the copy. Your last line is, "Try it. You'll love what it does to your clothes!" Do you just stand there? No. Action: You smell the towel one last time, you rub the towel next to your face to show how soft it is. Or, action: You give the detergent to your roommate to try. Then you continue folding the rest of your great-smelling laundry, whistling (ain't life grand?)—just keep "living" it—until they say "Thank you" or "Cut."

You've developed a whole story with a beginning, middle, and ending. You've established the location of the scene; set it up physically; decided who you are, what person you're talking to, and what your relationship is; chosen actions; established what you are doing before you start talking and what you are doing after the words end. You've visualized your whole scene. You've developed your own little play.

Exercise

Take the copy you analyzed in the first exercise on page 54 and decide:

1. Who are you? Since you don't have a casting director to tell you, given your physical type and age, make a choice. In other words, if you are a thirty-year-old, blonde, sophisticated-looking person, don't choose to be a blue-collar plumber. Remember, the copy will give you much of the information you need.

Once you've decided who you are, determine:

2. the physical space.
3. whom you're talking to.
4. relationships and imaginary characters.
5. what you're doing before you start talking.
6. what you will do after you finish talking.
7. what actions you will play.

Then visualize the whole scene. *Be very specific.* The stronger and more specific your choices, the better the work. Do your choices contribute to the key message or take attention away from it?

OK. Now stand in front of a large mirror in your house or set up your camcorder and try delivering the copy with your choices. Of course, you will have to talk to yourself if you're using a mirror. Talk to yourself as if you are your best friend. In other words, it is you talking, but talk to your image in the mirror as if it's your best friend whom you're trying to convince. Don't "watch" yourself. Analyze your choices after you do the exercise, not while you're doing it. The best choice is the camcorder if you have one. If all you have is a mirror, this will work too.

How did you feel? Were your choices simple and specific? Did they enhance the message of the commercial? Did you have a complete scene with a beginning, middle, and ending? Did you visualize the whole scene? If you think you can make it better, make even more specific choices and try it again. Or make another entire set of choices with the same copy. Be flexible, creative, and quick. These are requirements for successful acting in television commercials.

Remember, acquiring the techniques to become a good commercial actor is a step-by-step process. You will not be great after one or two exercises, or even after one or two weeks or months. It takes time and practice. The more you work at it, consistently, the better you will get, particularly if you are working with a good instructor. So don't get too critical of yourself now. Just keep working at it and improving, one step at a time.

On-Camera Techniques $\Big|$ 9

*I*n this chapter we are going to take a close look at on-camera techniques used by professional actors. When successfully incorporated, these techniques will dramatically improve your caliber as on-camera actors. You may already have learned some of them in your theatre acting training. You can practice each of these techniques one at a time with a commercial from Appendixes A–D. When you feel pleased with what you're doing, go to the next one. Let's begin with hitting your mark.

Hitting Your Mark

When you go into an audition, you will be asked to *go to your mark*. This is the spot marked on the floor with tape in front of the camera. Stand with your toes just touching it. After the introductions, go straight to your mark. Don't wait to be asked. This shows you are ready to begin work.

The location of the mark at an audition has been determined by the casting director based on where the lights and camera are focused. You may be asked to stand in one place to deliver the copy, or you may be asked to incorporate movement. If you are asked to improvise the movement, determine the boundaries with the casting director before your rehearsal. This is to make sure you are in adequate lighting and within the camera's range. It is always best to keep the range of your movements to a minimum.

When you are on a shoot, you will be asked to go to your first mark to begin the action and end up on your second or last mark (if there are more than two). This is called *hitting your mark.* I always go through the action of hitting my mark before I do a rehearsal with the camera. Then I know what to expect. The camera assistant will ask you to stand on your final mark first so he can measure the distance from the camera to your face and adjust the camera focus and lighting. When this is finished, you immediately return to your first mark to begin the take.

Since your mark is on the floor and you can't look down to find it during the scene, what do you do? Here are tricks to help you hit your mark every time. First, you can count the number of steps it takes to get from your first mark to your second. Or you can use other props or people in the scene to measure when to stop; for example, a chair arm, a doorway, or a window. If you have to move to another actor who is stationary, that person is your mark. Practice hitting your mark by:

- starting at your first mark and counting the steps to your last mark,
- then walking backwards from your last mark to your first mark,
- walking forward to your last mark, saying the lines as you go,
- and repeating it all a few times until you're comfortable with the movement.

Don't forget that any physical action you are directed to take must look as if it comes naturally from your impulses, not from a stage direction. Find a reason in your actions to justify the move. This is always the challenge of the on-camera actor, since you must move where you are directed to move. Playing an action is the best choice for making your movements believable.

Slating

Slating is the process of verbally identifying yourself by saying your name into the camera. When filming or taping, each shot or take is also identified with a slate (a clapboard or chalkboard with the scene number, take number, name of the commercial, director, and so forth written on it). Your slate is the first thing the client sees. Actors often forget the magnitude of the impact the slate has as part of the audition. As soon as the camera is rolling, you are auditioning. If the camera is turned on and you are not prepared for the slate, you will be seen doing whatever it is you're doing. Imagine being captured looking nervous, reading the copy over, sighing, or yawning, instead of looking at the camera, smiling, ready to introduce yourself to the client.

I will never forget my first slate. I was at my first audition, in the presence of both the casting director and the client, and was trying to look confident. The casting director said, "Slate it, please." I'm sure I had a look of horror on my face, but I managed to say, "Excuse me?" She smiled and said, "Would you give us your name?" She was very supportive and didn't make me look like a jerk. Thank God! I will always be grateful to her.

As soon as you get into the audition studio, introduce yourself or say hello, give your picture and resume, hit your mark, and prepare for the slate by smiling into the camera with a warm, energetic smile, ready to say your name with pride. If you are in doubt, after a reasonable interval of time without instruction, ask if she wants you to slate first. Sometimes the casting person will want you to rehearse before the slate, sometimes after, sometimes not at all (unfortunately). In any case, you will get used to hearing the tape deck being turned on or seeing the red light glowing on the camera.

Sometimes the casting person or client may want to chat before the slate. Make sure you are friendly, natural, and smiling, and on your mark facing the camera, even though you are talking directly to the casting person.

The client wants to see the real you. It's vital to show your real personality in the slate and in your commercial audition, particularly the friendly, spontaneous, energetic parts. Remember, the audition starts the minute you walk into the room.

When slating, announce your name in a friendly way. Say, in your mind, "Hi, I'm glad to be here!" while out loud you are saying "Hi, I'm Pat Dougan." End your slate with a downward inflection. If you end in an upward inflection, it will sound as if you're asking, "Am I Pat Dougan?" Try it. You'll see what I mean. Enunciate your name. You're used to saying it. The client may be hearing it for the first time. Sometimes they ask for a final slate, after you've done your read.

After the slate, you will probably be instructed to go right into the copy. Remember, if you have not been offered a rehearsal before, ask for one.

Exercise

Actors tend to underestimate how tricky it is to do a good slate and just how important this first impression is.

1. Practice your slate at home in front of the mirror.
2. Try different inflections.
3. Repeat the slate a series of times, keeping it natural, honest, and energetic each time.
4. *Always smile while slating.*
5. Are you feeling confident as you introduce yourself?

Holding the Copy Up, Out, and in Front

In the larger markets casting directors consistently provide cue cards at auditions. In other areas you will use hand-held copy. Be sure to *hold the copy up, out, and in front,* between your face and the camera lens. Hold it at a height and distance that is comfortable and allows you to *move your eyes only* to talk the copy. Don't hold it to the left or right of your face but directly out in front. If the copy is not held high enough, you will bob your head up and down. Naturally, the client wants to see your face, not the top of your head.

I was at an audition today and had the opportunity to read with several actors. Consistently, whether experienced or inexperienced, no actor held the copy up, out, and in front. Each one laid the copy on the table so when he had to look for a line, all you could see was the top of his head. One of the experienced actors was particularly good, but we saw more of his bald spot than his eyes. Finally, the director asked one of the less experienced actors to hold the copy up. For the first time, you could see this actor's eyes and face. It made all the difference in the world.

Occasionally, it seems appropriate to leave the copy on the table, in a casual kind of scene, or if you feel you really have it memorized. If you want to do this, look down with your eyes only to pick up the next line, not with your whole head.

It may feel unnatural at first to hold the copy up, out, and in front, but it will keep your face in the camera, and as you do it more and more you will become more comfortable with it. See Figure 9–1.

If you are a shaker, as most of us are, put a piece of matte board (like what you use for mailing your headshots) or some other light, sturdy object under the copy to help hold it still.

If there is blank space on the top of the page before the copy begins, fold that section down so that the copy you're reading is nearer to the top of the page. This way, your eye has less distance to travel from the copy to the camera.

Framing

I always ask how I am being framed, at auditions and on the job. *Framing* is the size of the shot. The three major kinds of framing are a close-up, a medium shot, and a long shot, with variations of each. A close-up (CU) is a tight shot of the head and shoulders. A medium close-up (MCU) or medium shot (MS) shows more than the close-up does. It goes down as far as your chest or your waist. A long shot (LS) captures your whole body; it is sometimes called a wide shot.

Why do I ask how I am being framed? Because the size of the work is dictated by the size of the frame. If you are framed in a CU, your work must be more subtle than if you are framed in a LS. I have had students framed in a CU who were gesturing and moving outside the frame because they assumed they were in a MS.

At first, you may not know how to adjust the subtleties of the size of your work. Through seeing playbacks in classes and practicing on your own, you will learn the correct adjustments. The actions are the same. The size of the expressions is altered.

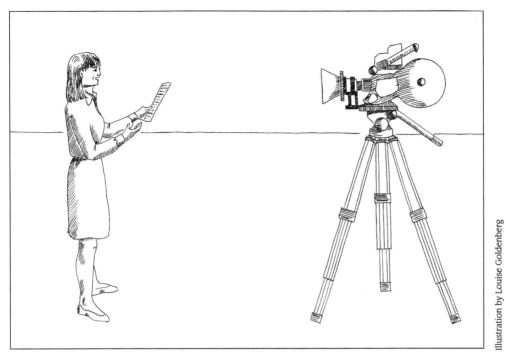

Illustration by Louise Goldenberg

Figure 9–1 Holding copy up, out, and in front

Feet Apart

When you are stationary, talking directly to the camera, give yourself a wide base of support. Spread your *feet apart.* This will keep you from swaying or shifting your weight from foot to foot. Most actors don't realize they do these things until they see themselves on playback. Naturally, your feet won't show on-camera since most auditions are framed in a medium to tight shot.

Try not to wear high-heeled shoes or boots. They can cause you to lose your balance.

The Pie Wedge

When you are talking to a real or imaginary person on-camera, always try to place that person (or your focus) within one foot of the camera on either side. This area is what I call the *pie wedge.* See Figure 9–2.

The purpose of the pie wedge is to keep your face mostly toward the camera. Never place a person directly to your right or left, unless you're directed to do so, since this will reveal only your profile. Always be aware of being "seen" by the camera.

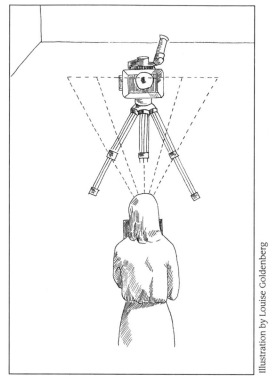

Figure 9–2 The Pie Wedge

Playing Out Toward Camera

Playing to the camera means talking directly to one person in the camera. *Playing out toward camera* is different. You are working out toward but not to the camera. You are playing your action and the camera captures you, in your own unself-conscious space. The camera catches you in this private moment. It's as if the camera isn't there, but you have to play out toward it to be captured by it. As the actor, you know you are being captured, but as the character, you are unaware that the camera is there. An example would be when you are alone, talking on the phone. Or when you have just been served a new food at home, by your wife, and your reaction is captured by the camera. The camera catches you in this private moment. It's as if the camera weren't there, but you have to play out toward it to be captured by it.

Exercise

1. Have an imaginary phone conversation. Use a real telephone for a prop.
2. Pick a spot on the wall where the camera would be.

3. Let your eyes do what they will. Sometimes they will focus on a particular place, sometimes they will wander.
4. Do not look at the camera, but be aware that it can see your face and eyes at all times. You are being captured by the camera in your own private space.
5. Put the experience from this exercise in your memory bank. The next time you have an audition or job and are requested to play *out toward* but not *to* the camera, revisit this memory and use it.

Talking The Copy

Most commercials are intended to make the viewers believe they are watching real people in real-life situations. You have to sound and look natural, not as if you're reading copy. This makes you believable. Some commercials are written non-conversationally and stiffly, but it is your job to sound natural and conversational while selling the product. The key is *talking the copy* rather than reading it. Of course, in real life we are rarely asking a good friend to buy a product. Be that as it may, your delivery must sound as if you are having a natural conversation with your good friend, talking with the words of the copy.

Energy

While you are being natural and sounding conversational, it is still vital to *keep energy in your work*. Here is the route theatre actors often take when transferring their skills to on-camera. First, their work is too big and overenunciated. They are playing the last row of the theatre. Then they learn how to be conversational and natural, but the work is too laid back, without any energy. Adding energy means adding intensity. You can have energy and be conversational and believable at the same time.

Exercise

First, use this exercise to achieve "talking" the copy. Try stringing the words together, just as we do in natural conversation. Then, make sure your style not only appears natural but has energy.

Here are some hints.

1. Throw away the idea of "performing" or "acting" the copy.
2. Ask a friend, family member, or actor friend to have this conversation (talking the copy) with you.
3. Improvise the copy. Ask her to have a conversation with you about the product.

4. Let her ask you questions about it. Explain the features of the product, the highlights. Talk about how great you think it is.
5. Your goal is to get across the basic message and key points of the commercial while having a natural conversation with your friend.
6. For now, don't worry about sticking strictly to the written words. Play around with it.
7. Once you feel comfortable with the give and take and naturalness of this improvised conversation, return to the actual words on the page.
8. Incorporate anything you found useful from the improvisation.
9. Keep it conversational by running the words together, as in real conversation, rather than overenunciating.
10. Don't start "acting" just because you're using the words of the copy. Try it. Make it flow.

Finally, are you talking the copy with purpose and energy?

Memorization

Should you *memorize* for the audition or not? I have observed countless students who think they have the commercial completely memorized, but then are consistently undone by their nerves. They just don't believe they need the copy in front of them until it's not there. Be very familiar with the commercial, but do not unrealistically stretch your memory. If there is a lot of copy, learn it by the different ideas or points. Since you are choosing strong "I want to . . ."s, it will be easier to get really comfortable with it.

Always hold the copy or refer to it on the cue card. No one expects you to have it memorized. The client does, however, want to see your face in the camera more than on the page. At the audition, have the opening and closing lines memorized so you are looking directly into the camera and leaving a good first and last impression. Otherwise, be very familiar with it, rehearse it well, but use the copy. It is also important to talk the copy exactly as written, doing no improvising unless requested.

On the job you must have the copy completely memorized as written. When I was starting out, I would think I had the copy memorized. Then I'd get on the set, and with the pressures and distractions plus the physical action in the commercial, I'd find that the copy wasn't as second nature to me as I had hoped. Then there are the further complications of not getting the copy until you arrive on the set. Or getting the copy in advance and having it totally memorized only to find it has been rewritten once you get there. Reprogramming your brain for slightly new lines can be a mind-bender. Always be prepared to make changes. Stay flexible.

Once you have the copy memorized, say it out loud many times. *Don't ever do an audition or job without talking the copy out loud first.* This may involve finding a private space in the lobby, hallway, or rest room. If you are doing a dialogue, ask someone to do it with you out loud once you feel you have it memorized. Although she will not be your acting partner the day of the shoot, you will be used to having someone to interact with, rather than just covering up her lines on the page as you memorize silently. Working out loud with a friend will also help you to learn your cues. If you have the storyboard or are aware of your planned physical action, do it while you are saying the lines. The ultimate test for me is saying the copy aloud while doing my physical action and having the television turned on at medium volume. If you can stand that distraction, you've got it memorized. Be very prepared and stay flexible. I always try to go into an audition or work situation with a "Yes!" attitude. Yes, I can! Because you just never know what might come up. And things always change.

Product Name

When in doubt, *always ask how the product name is pronounced.* The client will not be happy if you mispronounce it. This is a totally acceptable and smart practice. It shows you're professional.

Give the product name special emphasis, just as you do with key words and phrases, and smile if it's appropriate. Pause just a moment before the product name, or give it special emphasis by saying it as if it had quotation marks around it. As a spokesperson, always be looking at the camera, not on the page or cue card, when you say the product name.

Face and Body Expression

Since television commercials are a visual medium, we need to be able to see your choices. Once you've made your "I want to . . ." choices, you have to show those choices with *face and body expression.* And if you're really trying to get something from the person you're talking to, it will show in your face. You should not look as if you were directed to put on an expression. You must look completely natural. If your choices are weak or flabby or if you don't really believe in your choices, the expressions will not show in your face and body. They will look phony.

You will recall, the size of your expressions is dictated by the framing of the shot. If you are framed in a close-up, your expressions will be more subtle than if you are framed in a wider shot.

Some of my students are totally convinced their faces show their choices. They may have wonderful vocal expression, but nothing much is showing in their faces. When they see themselves on-camera, they can't believe it. The theatre-trained students have the opposite problem—too much expression. They tend to play to the last row of the theatre, and sometimes their choices aren't grounded or real.

At first, to help facilitate "showing" your intentions and, as a result, your feelings, make your three "I want to . . ." changes *between* the lines, not on the lines themselves. Make deliberate choices. Ultimately you will want to make spontaneous "I want to . . ." choices all through the copy. But for now, deliberately make three choices between the lines, when the subject changes. Of course, you can't lollygag around in the space between subject changes. You have to plan out your "I want to . . ."s and make the changes quickly and pointedly. You don't have time to cruise into it. (Remember, it's all timed.) You want to set your goal toward having the skill and facility to make the changes in a millisecond, concisely. And all of this must show primarily in your face and also in your body (if the framing includes your body).

Why is it important to make three different changes? Because *these changes provide contrast in the commercial.* Without contrast, the whole thing will be monotonous and boring. The viewer won't know what he's supposed to remember.

Exercise

In this exercise, your face and body are your only sources of expression. There are no words or sound. You will be able to see how well your choices are showing in your face. This works best if you can do it with another person. If possible, tape it on-camera.

1. Ask the person to stand next to the camera so your face is captured in the picture.
2. Let's say you pick "I want to soothe you" as an action.
3. Now have a *silent* conversation with the person.
4. Make a personal commitment to make her feel better. You may be saying things in your mind like "Did you have a bad day? What can I do for you? Can I bring you your slippers? A cup of tea? I'm really sorry things aren't going well."
5. Do it all silently. Your actions will show in your face. The trick here is to really play the action, and not just put on a face. Your work always has to be honest.

Pacing

Another way to provide variety and contrast is to alter the *pacing.* Some parts of the commercial need to be said more slowly than other parts. Since the product name and the key points need to be emphasized, the pacing may be slower on these parts. However, less important sections, like lists of attributes of the product, can often be said more quickly.

If you speak the copy all at the same pace, there will be no variety. Alter the pacing to emphasize the key points, just as we do in real life. At the same time, keep the copy flowing. Don't allow your pacing to make the copy choppy or disjointed. Remember, every commercial is precisely timed. Finally, as you increase the pacing don't lose the specific choices in your work.

Exercise

1. Choose a commercial from Appendixes A–D.
2. After you understand the key message, record it on a tape recorder or on-camera all at the same pace. If you emphasize key words or the product name, don't slow down. Maintain an even pace.
3. Now, decide what information or phrases are less important.
4. Choose which sections of the copy you will speed up.
5. Record the copy again and listen back. Hear the difference? You may want to make more pacing alterations and read it again. If you can clearly hear the key message when you play it back, then your alterations are on the mark. If not, rethink your choices and try the exercise again.

Pitch and Inflections

Use of *pitch and inflections* is important to provide variety. Pitch is the tone of your voice. Inflection is changing the pitch or tone. In the everyday world, we speak with rising and falling inflections. We don't talk in a monotone (on a single tone), or in a singsong pattern (with exactly the same pattern of inflection for each and every sentence). In real life, we talk at many different pitch levels with rising and falling inflections. Likewise, when you are acting in a commercial, you want to have the same kind of vocal variety. You want to sound "natural" with energy.

Exercise

How do you make sure you speak with varied pitch and inflections? First you need to *hear* how you sound in real life.

1. Record a real-life conversation with a family member, coworker, or fellow student. Explain what you're doing.
2. Decide on a topic to discuss. Forget the tape recorder. Just have a normal conversation. Don't act! Be yourself.
3. Listen to it. Does your voice rise and fall naturally? Or do you detect a problem? Are you speaking in a monotone, with everything on the same pitch? Or do all your sentences end with an upward or downward inflection rather than some of both?

If you detect a problem:

4. Name your problem as you hear it.
5. Do the opposite of your problem. For example, if you end too many sentences with an upward inflection—which makes you sound as if you're always asking a question—deliberately end all your sentences with a downward inflection on the next read. (For assistance, mark your copy in pencil with arrows going up or down.) Or if you speak in a monotone, mark your copy in specific places with upward and downward arrows for inflections.
6. Read and record the copy this new way.

Change begins once you *hear* the problem.

7. Finally, re-record the copy a third time, integrating some of both patterns.

Be aware that problems with pitch and inflection are part of your daily speaking patterns and take persistent and regular practice to change.

Smiling

You need to be able to *smile* with ease while talking and listening. Watch TV. Actors spend a lot of time smiling in commercials. Warm, friendly, inviting. Naturally, if the copy is intended to be serious, you adjust accordingly. And it's not natural to be smiling constantly. But it's important to be able to smile a good deal of the time. Many of my students think they are smiling when they are not. They say, "I *am* smiling!" Then they see themselves in playback and say, "It felt as if I were smiling, but it sure doesn't look that way."

How do you smile for a period of time while you're talking? Walk around your house or apartment with the goal of smiling while talking for at least three minutes. Pick a subject that encourages smiling. Have a conversation with another person or tell her a story. Be sincere. And really smile, don't just half smile. This exercise will prove that you can smile for a consistent length of time while talking. You need to be comfortable with this since you will be smiling much of the time in commercials. Try it in the mirror. Do you believe yourself?

The Living Freeze

When you come to the end of the copy in an audition or on the job, it's important to keep the action or the freeze alive. You keep the freeze alive by ending the physical action of the scene while keeping your face (and thoughts) alive. Do this by simultaneously moving your head ever so slightly and keeping your final attitude alive with active thoughts going through your mind. This is all done without sound. Don't just stop and freeze everything, or you will look like a mannequin. Keep smiling (if appropriate), breathing, and moving ever so slightly while you continue with active thoughts until the director says "Cut" or "Thank you." Thus, the *living freeze.*

Cue Cards

Cue cards are large, white, poster-size cards on which the commercial is printed in large letters. They are used in the larger and medium-sized markets for most auditions. Cue cards are placed right next to the camera so your eye simply travels from cue card to lens. Remember, cue cards are just that—for cueing, not for reading the whole copy. As with hand-held copy, your eyes should be in the camera the majority of the time.

Actors love to use cue cards because it frees them up from holding the copy. Your face is always seen. And your hands are free for gesturing or using props.

What are some of the tricks for effectively using cue cards? I've learned quite a number of them from my own work and from watching my students.

1. Keep your face and body towards the camera, not towards the cue card. You're not talking to the cue card.
2. Move your eyes only from card to lens; don't move your head or body.
3. Ask for an out loud rehearsal before doing the first take. You will be seeing the copy written on the cue card for the first time. Prior to entering the audition room, you have only seen the copy on the page. The copy may be formatted differently on the cue card than it was on the page.
4. Determine, during the out-loud rehearsal, at what points in the copy you need to return to the cue card. Always keep your eyes on the camera for the opening and closing and while saying the product name.
5. Don't drop character when looking for your next line. If you get lost, stay in character until you find your place. (It may seem to you that ten minutes have passed, but in reality it's only been a few seconds.)
6. When working with another person, always read and be familiar with the whole copy, not just your lines. When you're working in doubles and the third person in the scene is the camera, try to pick up the beginning of your next line while your partner is talking. Attempt to cheat, with your eyes only, to the cue card rather than with your head or body. Don't "hang" on the cue card. Pick up your cue and then move your focus back to your partner. After all, you are supposed to be having a conversation with your partner.
7. It is best to have the cue card to the right of the camera (from your viewpoint). In this position, there is less distance for your eye to travel to the camera. (You may not be able to control this position.)
8. If you need glasses to see the cue cards, seriously consider contact lenses. The glasses "look" should be an option rather than a necessity.

Writing the copy on cue cards is a real art. Few people do it well. Ideally, it's in capital letters with black ink, evenly spaced. Be mentally prepared for all kinds of variations. You won't get to see the card until you're in the audition room, but sometimes just knowing it may be tough to read the card psychologically prepares you.

Microphones

This technique is simple. Ignore the *microphone.* Speak as if it weren't there, just like real life. Remember—natural with energy.

Props

When using *props* at an audition, keep these guidelines in mind:

- Whenever possible, use a prop or facsimile where the copy indicates. There is always something available in the room or out of your pocket or purse.
- Rule of thumb: keep it simple. The commercial should not be about how many times you use the prop. You may want to bring it in to establish it and then take it out at some point, or keep it in the whole time. Make a decision when to use it. If the commercial is just as effective without the prop, don't use it.
- As a spokesperson, hold the prop out in front of you, never past either shoulder. As a rule, keep it out in front and just to the right of your face. It may seem as if you are covering your face. But, what *feels* natural to you and what *looks* natural on-camera will vary. Practice in the mirror or on-camera to find a good position. Actors tend to hold the prop too far from their faces.
- Hold the product so the name shows to the camera. You don't need to see it; the viewer does.
- When bringing the prop into the frame, briefly look at it. Otherwise, it will appear to have a life of its own.
- In a slice-of-life or quick-cut, use the prop naturally, making sure the camera can see you.

Cheat

When working with another actor, *cheat* your body and face out to camera. Don't get caught completely in profile. We want to see your face and eyes. You may need to talk to your partner while looking at a spot on the wall near her eyes. The impulse will be to look at your partner. Of course it's always easier to have a conversation when you're looking directly at the person. But you want to be seen by the camera.

Also, always stand or sit on the same horizontal level with your partner, so you are not upstaging or being upstaged. Practice these techniques with someone before you try them at an audition or on a job.

Spontaneity

With all these techniques and rules, how do you ever make it look *spontaneous?* While you're learning and applying these techniques, it probably won't be very spontaneous. That's the purpose of classes—to have a work space where you can take chances, make mistakes, and see growth. It's difficult to practice new techniques for the first time at an audition or on the job. Eventually, with consistent practice, these techniques will get cemented in your brain. They will become instinctive. The goal is to look as if you're doing this for the very first time—spontaneously.

After you've done all your preparation and before you enter the audition room, take a moment to clear your head. Take three deep breaths and say to yourself, "I'm going to do this as if it were the first time I'd ever done it."

Claim the Space

When you get into the audition room, *claim the space.* This is your space and your time. Act as if you belong there. Look confident even if you're nervous. You want to be there. You own the space for this short time. Transferring your visualization helps you to claim the space because you have a "picture" of who everyone is in your scene and where they are.

Now, give it your best. That's all you can ask of yourself.

Naturally, these techniques take time to learn and use effectively. It's always extremely important to conduct yourself as a professional in the audition process. Let's look at some helpful audition techniques and etiquette.

Audition Techniques and Etiquette | *10*

O nce you've started marketing yourself on a steady and regular basis, with any luck, you will start getting calls for auditions from agents or casting directors. What are the appropriate questions and answers when you're called in to audition? You want to be as prepared and professional as you can, so getting the proper amount of information at the time of the call is very important.

The Phone Call

When you are called by your agent or a casting director to audition for a commercial, the person calling you will give you certain critical information about the audition and the job. There may be other things you need to know, too. Since the person is calling quite a large number of other actors for the same audition, sometimes helpful information gets left out. This is not deliberate. Casting people are only human and get tired, too.

Here is a checklist of helpful questions to ask when you receive the call:

1. Date and time of the audition.
2. Location. Sometimes the audition is somewhere other than the casting director's office. It may be at the ad agency or a production company.
3. What is the product in the commercial? What are you selling?

4. Is this a union or nonunion job? If you are a union member, you should not be called for nonunion work and *cannot* do nonunion work!
5. What character or type are you playing?
6. Where is the character in the copy—grocery store, home, office? This will help you determine how to look—what to wear and how to fix your hair. (Casting people usually describe the characters by saying something like "This person is a regular, middle-class guy working on his lawn," or "This person is an upscale professional in the office, or a middle-class mom at home, or a blue-collar construction worker on the job." Select your wardrobe accordingly.
7. Is there copy? Do I have lines? Or is it an improvisation?
8. Will there be cue cards for the audition?
9. What is the date of the shoot? If you are already booked for a job on that date, tell the casting person now. He may or may not ask you to come to the audition anyway. (What is *first refusal?* It is a request by a producer for you to hold a particular date open for a job. If you receive another job offer for the same date, you will need to call the first producer and tell him you have an offer for the same date. If the first producer wants to book you, then call the second producer and tell her you are booked for that date. If you are called in by an agent, tell her and she will handle it. This also applies to conflicts where you are appearing in a competing product commercial. You cannot audition or accept a job for a competing product if you are playing a principal role in a commercial that is being aired or that you are being paid for while on hold for future broadcast. As I've said before, if you don't mention your conflict or first refusal up front, and you get the job and can't do it, you will be in big trouble. Some casting people mistakenly say you are "on hold" rather than "first refusal." *On hold* means you are booked for the job—you've been hired. See the Glossary.)
10. Whether you're called by a casting director (who works for the client) or an agent (who works for you), make sure you know what kind of commercial it is: local, regional, national, dealer, or test-market. (Casting directors and agents always tell you.) This will tell you what you will be paid for the session fee at scale. In some markets you may be paid above scale if you or your agent negotiates it. For commercials that run for extended periods, you will continue to earn residuals beyond your original session fee. Sometimes you are booked for a national or a test-market spot and it doesn't end up going national or being tested after all, so don't get your hopes up for making more money until you get the check in your hand. For all union jobs, you are guaranteed the minimum fee for any booking less your agent's ten percent fee. (In some states and under the commercials and other union contracts, such as theatrical and television, agents are not allowed to take their fees out of scale. The ten percent must be above scale. Check with your local union office to be sure.)
11. If you are nonunion, you absolutely need to inquire about the pay when you are called to audition. Since you have no union protection, you also need to find out how and when you will be paid if you get the job. Don't

be embarrassed about this! There isn't a good businessperson in the world who doesn't establish, up front, the conditions of her employment.
12. If the location of the audition is completely foreign to you and you don't have any idea how to get there, ask for directions and a phone number of a contact person at the location of the audition.

In general, keep your questions succinct. Your agent or the casting director is a busy person. Don't keep her on the phone endlessly, asking for advice or chatting. Ask your questions, thank her, and hang up.

Preparation for the Audition

It's a good idea to review your on-camera techniques on a regular basis, from this book and from any courses you've taken. More often than not, you won't get the opportunity to audition as much as you'd like. We all get rusty. So it's important to keep tuned by practicing commercial copy at home or in classes. If you practice on a regular basis, it will increase your confidence. If you wait until the night before the audition, you won't feel as confident as if you've been practicing steadily or auditioning regularly. Make your life easier by practicing out loud, in front of the mirror, at least two or three times each week.

Exercise

A day or two before the audition, think through how your character would dress and look.

1. Select your *wardrobe.* Put it on. Does it do the trick for the character you will be playing? There is no one "right" look. In addition, will the colors and patterns (if there are any) be OK on-camera? Have you chosen pastels or fairly neutral, solid colors? Do your clothes enhance your character rather than distract? Make any adjustment you feel you need. Also, plan to bring a few enhancements to the audition, such as a jacket, sweater, bow tie, necktie, hair combs, and elastics. This will protect you in case you find the character is somewhat different than you thought or were told.
2. Fix your *hair.* Make it look neat, in place, and manageable. Make it fit into your character.
3. Next, have you been happy with your *makeup?* Do you need to use a bit more blush for color, a little less eye makeup, or a little base to cover your beard shadows? According to casting director Maura Tighe of Tighe Chase Casting in Boston, women new to the business often make the mistake of using too much makeup. Men, if the audition is late in the day, will you need to plan to shave right beforehand? Men may also want to lightly cover puffy eyes.

4. What about *jewelry?* Wear none or keep it extremely simple. Remember, they want to see you, not your jewelry. A watch is OK. Only stud earrings, women, or nothing at all.
5. OK. Now you've got your "look" together. Now it's time to *practice some copy.* Pick a piece of copy from the back of the book.
6. Next, *review the exercises* in Chapters 5 and 6 on "Understanding the Copy" and "Defining Your Character." Once you've done those two exercises, making strong, specific choices, choose a second, different interpretation for the same commercial.

As I've said, many times the director will ask you to try a "different read" and will not designate what he wants that to be. So you must be prepared to give him a different interpretation, based on choosing active "I want to . . ."s. (Remember the difference between a "conspiratorial" and "playful" read?)

7. *Choose from your "I want to . . ." list,* to excite him, to thrill her, embarrass her, make him feel guilty, tease him. Make strong, positive choices—active verbs that you can "play."
8. *Practice the copy* in the mirror, talking to yourself. Tape the copy next to the mirror at eye level, to simulate using a cue card. Or mark a spot on the wall for the camera and tape the "cue card" to the right of it to practice. Make sure you believe what you're doing. Be spontaneous and believable.
9. Now, give yourself permission to *have a good time at the audition.* You won't be perfect. No one ever is. It takes time to build confidence and skill. Go in with confidence and do the best you can. You will get better the more you work and practice.

The Day of the Audition

THE WARM-UP

It's a very good idea to do a physical and vocal warm-up before your audition. You can do this at home; or if you are coming from a job or some other location, you can arrive at the audition ten minutes earlier than planned (thirty minutes before your call time). Find a place out in the hall or the bathroom. From your theatre training and classes, you will have developed a set of warm-up exercises. Do them. Don't disrupt a whole office. But there are some loosening up exercises you can do without making much sound. Be sure to breathe. Do some sighing and vocal warm-ups. This will help channel your nerves.

WHEN YOU ARRIVE AT THE AUDITION

Now that you are properly prepared, it's time for the audition itself.

- Plan to arrive at least twenty minutes before your call time. How you conduct yourself as a businessperson is as important as how skilled you are as an actor. Of course, occasionally you will be tied up at another audition, so you may have to be a bit late. You should be sure to notify the casting director of this so she and her staff won't have to wait for you. Don't get them angry before you've had a chance to show them your stuff. Also, be prepared to wait much longer than expected before you audition. Auditions can take longer than scheduled.
- *Sign in* on the sign-in sheet. It will request any number of things, which may include name, address, phone number and/or contact phone number, your agent's name and phone number, union affiliations, the number of this audition (first, second, third), possibly your age, racial type, social security number, and any conflicts you have on the shoot date. The information on the sign-in sheet varies from market to market.
- *A casting assistant or CD will take a Polaroid picture of you and attach it to a size card.* You fill in your clothing sizes, which will be given to the wardrobe person should you get the job. With the Polaroid, you often don't have to give your headshot. But always have several with you, just in case.
- A casting assistant will give you the commercial copy and, if available, the storyboard. Or these may be lying next to the sign-in sheet. *Study the copy and storyboard.* The storyboard is your bible. It will show you what your character says and does when, where, and with whom. (The drawings of your character on the storyboard are often the art director's ideal character, having the "look"—the hair and clothes—as well as the point of view. Some actors take the chance of asking the casting director how the character in the storyboard is dressed as well as the hairdo. Most casting directors don't have time for this, so ask questions *selectively.*) Then take the copy and find a quiet place to begin your work. Be sure to stay within earshot of the casting person. He won't want to have to come look for you when it's your turn to audition.

You just practiced at home, so your on-camera techniques will be readily accessible to you when you have this new piece of copy.

- *Read the copy four or five times.* Every time you read it, you'll discover additional information.
- Next, *understand and analyze the copy.* What did the storyboard tell you about your character and your action? Make strong, active, playable choices ("I want to . . .").
- *Develop your whole scene* in keeping with the storyboard.
- Now start to *practice out loud,* quietly. No one will think anything of this. Actors do it all the time at auditions. Find a spot on the wall to focus on for the camera, hold your copy up, out, and in front, and begin to practice. Or find a quiet spot.

Once you feel secure with your first set of choices,

■ *choose a different interpretation* (more "hard sell" or more "conversational," and so forth) and another set of "I want to . . ." choices to go with that read. Don't change the scene or your character, per se. Do give your character a second strong set of objectives, and active, playable verbs, to show your diversity and skill as an actor. Remember, the director very well may ask you to do it another way. So you'll be all set.

Now you're ready to roll.

Don't disturb other actors or get involved in chitchat before your audition. You often run into old friends and acquaintances, and the energy level is pretty charged. There is that natural feeling of competition as well as wanting to catch up with other actors, so it can be very difficult to center yourself. Someone may want to chat with you while you want to prepare. It can be awkward. But try to disengage yourself by either making plans to meet after the audition or saying something like "It's good to see you. Can we chat after the audition? I haven't had a chance to look at the copy yet." Be polite and do your work. Actors understand this.

Some actors will do little or no preparation. Don't let this throw you off or make you think you don't need to prepare. Keep your stakes high. Do your work and get prepared.

Most casting offices are not soundproof, and you can disturb other actors' auditions while joking or chatting in the waiting room. Be considerate.

If you can, ask one of the actors coming out of the audition, or the casting assistant, for information: Is there a cue card? Who is in there besides the director? Were they nice? Or, how was it? How many times did they ask you to do it? Depending on what city you're working in, actors will be more or less helpful. In some cities, actors are very forthcoming with this information. In other places, they won't tell you much of anything because you are the competition to whom they could lose the job.

Should you be asked to audition before your actual call time, if you feel you are prepared, go for it. However, if you are not ready, do not feel obligated to go in before your time. Say something like "Gee, my call time is at 12:00, and I need a little more time." Then remove yourself from the immediate area, but stay within eye- and earshot, and continue to prepare.

Always try to maintain a sense of confidence and professionalism. Don't look or act desperate or too eager to please. This is a business. Even though all of us have to start at the beginning, you are a whole, complete person who also happens to be an actor. You should be treated with respect. Don't settle for less. Find positive ways to ensure that treatment.

You may be nervous. This is completely natural. Everyone is nervous some of the time, whether they look it or not. Some people cover their nervousness with toughness, or cockiness or by showing helplessness. But underneath it all, everyone is nervous sometimes. So don't get caught up in wondering why those other actors don't look nervous when you're dying inside. You have your goal, to prepare for the commercial. Stick with it. You couldn't have a clearer motivation. This will help you stay focused.

Now right before you go in to audition, do a few quick shoulder lifts and drops and take a few deep breaths to help break up any last-minute tensions. Focus yourself. Now you're ready.

The Audition

The first thing I do is try to assess the mood when entering the audition studio. Is the casting director, director, or client open to a direct introduction or are they tired and do they just want to get down to business? If the mood is inviting and friendly, I go up to the table where they're sitting and introduce myself. If the casting director has not already given them a picture and résumé, I offer my Polaroid and headshot at that time. Sometimes the casting director will introduce you automatically. Other times, it's up to you. If the mood is unfriendly or indifferent, I simply say "Hi" or "Hello" and *go to my mark.* Don't forget to smile. This all happens in just a few seconds.

You will be surprised how well you can pick up on the mood of an audition. It is an invaluable skill. Of course you will still go through the audition with confidence and dignity, no matter what the mood of the auditors; but this awareness helps you determine what is appropriate or inappropriate behavior when you are in a situation where the other people have the power to hire you. Again, whatever the mood, it should not change the basic you. Awareness of the mood simply helps you adapt to the situation. You are capable of doing a good audition whatever the situation. Don't take it personally if one of the auditors is in a bad mood. Don't get sidetracked by doubting yourself and wondering, "Why aren't they talking to me? Oh, God, they don't like me. I must be doing a terrible job." They don't have it in for you. It's probably just been a long day. Or maybe they had a fight with someone this morning.

In the unusual situation where the casting director wants to, *be prepared to chat.* He is usually looking for what you are like as a person, so try to be yourself. I have had a variety of auditions, particularly for films, where the director wants to chat. He'll say, "Tell me about yourself." He is probably looking for more than your credits. What are your interests outside the business? Or he may look at your résumé and see something to start a conversation about. You may both have worked with the same person on some other project. Be prepared to talk about yourself at any audition. Practice this out loud at home. It seems to be one of the more difficult things for actors to do unexpectedly at an audition, believe it or not, and some people are not adequately prepared for this surprise request.

The great thing about a friendly atmosphere is that it loosens up everybody, particularly you, and generally makes for a more successful audition. Since *the casting director and director are on your side and want you to do well,* they will do their best to make you comfortable. Believe it or not, they are not there to judge you. If you look good, they look good.

But, remember, they have been auditioning people all day and they get tired. Like the rest of us, they are only human.

Often the director will give you some information about the commercial, what the client is looking for, what kind of person your character is, the action of the commercial. If the direction you are given contradicts the choices you've made while rehearsing, so be it. The name of the game in commercial acting is adaptability. *You must be able to incorporate directions immediately.* What the director asks you to do will probably not be that far from some of the choices you've already made, so give it your best. If you don't understand a specific direction, ask for clarification.

As wonderful as some directors can be, some of them do not have an actor's vocabulary and give direction according to the results they want to see. It is your job to find the *process* to achieve that result.

It's too easy to try to fake on-camera, to *not* go through the process to get to the result. But let me tell you, it always shows when you're faking. So don't do it, even when you're stuck. Your job as an actor is to develop the technique necessary so you have a battery of active choices available to you in a moment. Commercial acting is about results. The director usually doesn't care how you get there as long as you get there, believably and skillfully. Eventually, you will choose actions automatically, without consciously choosing.

Sometimes the director won't give you any direction on the copy before your first take. That's OK because you've done your preparation and you're ready. *Be prepared to deliver the copy a different way.* Do be prepared to implement his direction, if given, on a second take. You're an actor. Stay flexible. Lighten up. It's only a commercial, it's not cancer.

Now you've gone to your mark. *If you are using a cue card, ask if you can read it down.* This means just what it says, reading down the copy on the cue card since you are seeing it in this format for the first time. When you do this, you are mentally marking the transition points from the hand-held copy to the cue card. Quickly read it down, quietly, out loud. Technically this is not a rehearsal since you are not rehearsing it the way you plan to do it for the first take.

Ask how you are being framed. It will help you determine the "size" of your work (smaller work for a tight shot, slightly larger work for a wide shot.)

Before you ask for a rehearsal, quickly transfer your visualization of how you've developed the whole scene outside the audition room. Where have you placed the other characters in the scene? Are they in the camera? Do you need to place or actually use any essential objects or a prop? Do you need to transfer the visualization of a room or particular environment? Do this very quickly, in just a few seconds. The auditors don't want to wait for you to "create." Don't talk about it, just do it. Now, *claim the space as your own.* This is your scene, your space. You belong here. Don't look as if you're visiting or forced to be here.

If it is not offered, *ask for a rehearsal.* In my particular geographic market, I have noticed that in the last three years, rehearsals have not been automatically granted. This is a real shame. Although the casting people may be constantly under the gun for time, working without a rehearsal makes it tough for an actor to give her best. Consequently, it shortchanges the client. It is in everybody's best interest to give the actor a rehearsal. It makes everybody look good. However, we don't make the rules. I have a director friend who prefers not to give a rehearsal. He feels actors are more spontaneous as a result and some good stuff is generated. However, he gives the actor three takes at an audition, one to see what you come up with and two more to implement his direction. In my opinion, however, a rehearsal helps the actor work out the kinks.

If you are not offered a rehearsal, try to charm or humor the casting director or director into giving you one, unless the mood is unfriendly—then simply ask, "Can we rehearse one?" It may or may not work. If you are not granted a rehearsal and are only given one take and feel you didn't do what you wanted, ask for another take. However, be *certain* you can do it better on the second take. In any case, with or without a rehearsal, you will do your best.

Here goes your first take. Since you've memorized them, *deliver the first and last lines directly into the camera.*

The casting director or director may say thank you or may ask you to do another take. It is relatively common to do two takes. If asked to do another, I say, "Was that close to what you're looking for?" or "Do you have any suggestions?" If you are finished after one take, the director may have seen what he needed to see. One take may be all he has given anyone. You may have done the first take so well, he doesn't need to see more. He may feel you're not quite what he's looking for in terms of type, and on and on. There are as many possibilities as there are actors. So don't torture yourself. You can speculate forever and never know why. So give it up. It will only make you crazy.

Casting directors and directors want to see how you take direction, since in commercial work you have to do take after take after take with consistency and energy. Are you adaptable? Can you implement directions quickly? Are you an easy person to work with? Are you likable? For these reasons, you will often be given a second take. Listen carefully to the directions. The CD or director is on your side. He wants you to do well. If you are unclear about the direction, ask for clarification. If the direction is still unclear, give it your best shot and do it the way you think he wants it done. When you succeed, you will make both of you look good.

Sometimes after a first take, the CD or director will say, "Try it for me another way," Of course you have a second read all prepared, so this will make you look good. Many actors will not have done this preparation, and their second take will look pretty much like the first take.

Do not ever, under any circumstances, apologize, visually or verbally, for your work!!!

After everyone has said thank you and you have crisply exited the audition room, be nice to yourself. Don't beat yourself up. You did the best you could. Congratulate yourself for that. Remember that with each audition, you are *building relationships* with the CDs and directors. You will get other auditions with them.

Of course there are always areas for improvement. Later in the day you can assess two or three areas you want to improve upon for your next audition. But for now, give yourself a pat on the back. Ask if you can take the copy with you, in case there's a callback. Some CDs in New York make you sign an agreement *not* to take the copy.

Commercial acting is a series of acquired techniques and skills. Your skills will improve the more you work at it and practice and study. In the commercial classes I teach with theatre-trained actors, after twenty-five hours the actors know they are just grasping the basics. It takes patience.

Exercise

1. At home after the audition, pick one or two specific points or techniques that you would like to improve upon at the next audition.
2. Take the copy you just auditioned for. Stand in front of your mirror, and add those one or two points or techniques.
3. After you've worked on it awhile and you think you've successfully incorporated these techniques, write them down so you can remind yourself before your next audition.
4. Then, after the next audition, add one or two new areas for improvement.

This way you will continue to get better and better, and you will have a written list of improvements, which should help you feel good about yourself and should also act as a reminder for future auditions.

The Callback

Ninety-eight percent of the time, there are *callbacks* for commercials—sometimes more than one callback. The audition is generally conducted by the CD, and the callback is conducted by the director with the client present. The callback is usually the first time you see the director and client. They like how you looked and what you did at the audition. There are two things going on at the callback: first, the client and director want to make sure they are "on the same page," that they are going in the same direction with the commercial; and second, they want to see how well you take direction, what you bring to the party in terms of choices and flexibility.

Since the first audition, the storyboard and copy may also have changed. The callback, as well as on the job, is where your skills and techniques are so important. Be ready and able to make quick changes in your work. I've heard a director say that this actor was great at the audition, but he couldn't repeat it at the callback. Or he couldn't implement new direction. Get any available feedback from the CD or agent when you are called for the callback. Did the director or client request any changes? Does he want to see you do something different, specifically? How has the commercial changed or evolved? Any other thoughts?

Don't try to just repeat or imitate what you did at the first audition. Your work will be dead. Keep it fresh and spontaneous. Play actions.

Wear the same clothes and hair that you wore to the first audition, unless you are requested to make a change. This helps the auditors remember you from the first round.

They are looking for your range of interpretations and deliveries. Never say, "I can't do that," unless you are asked to do a special skill such as snow skiing and you can't. *Be sure not to lie.* Be flexible, explore, and be fun to work with.

Now that your audition techniques are in order, let's look, in more detail, at the professional relationships you must develop and maintain with agents, casting directors and directors, and advertising agencies.

Agents, Casting Directors, Directors, and Ad Agencies

11

*I*n the process of auditioning and getting jobs you will be working with directors, casting directors, and advertising agencies. Depending on your geographic market, you may also be working with agents. Remember, you're continually building relationships with these people, whether or not you win a particular job.

Who Are They?

AGENTS

Agents work for and are paid by the actor. They will call their signed actors first. They may also call actors who freelance through them. Agents submit actors to casting directors.

It is the agent's job to know the skills and work of the actors who are signed or who freelance through them. The agent's income and reputation are contingent on the type and quality of actor he or she sends to the audition. If the agent sends actors who win the jobs, the agent makes money.

In New York and Chicago, you may be signed with one agent exclusively, or you can freelance through several. In Los Angeles, you must be signed by a commercial agent in order to be seen by a casting director. In the medium to smaller markets, freelancing is the norm.

Legitimate agents are licensed by each state. They are required to sign agreements as franchised agents with the actors' unions. They are paid a 10 percent commission of your earnings. (Your paycheck usually goes to the agency first. Then you get a check from the agency with the commission deducted, and a copy or stub from the original check.) If you decide to sign with an agent, make sure he or she is legitimate. Never do business with someone who requests payment in advance to get you work.

CASTING DIRECTORS

Commercial casting directors are either independent (own their own businesses) or work for advertising agencies. Although some of the larger ad agencies still have their own in-house casting directors, in the last few years many in-house CDs have been eliminated. Most casting directors for commercials these days are independent.

The casting director tells the agent the specific types she's looking for in the commercial, as well as the breakdown of the characters. Some examples of this are a thirty-five-year-old, blonde, middle-class dad (with a sore throat) skating with his ten-year-old daughter; a black business-woman, forty to forty-five, at an automatic teller machine; or a twenty-five to thirty-year-old male bodybuilder who can act *and* play Tarzan. The casting director may or may not provide the agent with the copy.

Your first audition is usually with the casting director or casting assis-tant. The callback is attended by the director, an ad agency person, and the client, or any combination of these.

ADVERTISING AGENCIES

Advertising agencies are the companies hired by the client (Kellogg, Ford, Smithkline Beecham) to develop, produce, and get the commercial aired for their product (Corn Flakes, Taurus, Sucrets). Ad agencies that produce broadcast advertising have account executives, copywriters, art directors, producers, and others who work with the client on conceiving, developing, and producing the commercial. At a certain point in that development, a director is hired to help evolve the creative process and shoot the commercial.

DIRECTORS

The director is the person who directs all aspects of filming the commer-cial, including you, the talent. You meet the director for the first time at the callback. The director may be a freelancer, have his or her own pro-duction company, or work as an employee for a production company.

How Do You Work With Them?

AGENTS

There are small agents who work solo, and there are large agencies that may have several different departments of agents, including commercial, television, film, theatre, models or "beauty," and "stars." In the 1980s, when the economy was booming and jobs were more abundant, many actors found it ideal to freelance through a number of agents in order to develop a working relationship with several before signing exclusively with one. However, in this economy, it generally makes more sense to be signed since your agent will send you out before the freelance actors. Agents also have established contacts that you may not have. There are varying opinions on when and whether to sign with an agent. You need to do adequate research in your city to decide. If you are in a city where the only work or the majority of the work is obtained through agents, you need to find an agent you like and can work with. Your relationship with your agent should be a *business partnership.* You are "hiring" the agent to represent you. You should not put all the business decisions of your career in your agent's hands. A good agent will want to establish with you where you want to go—your long-range goals—as well as boundaries and parameters to help *you* make good business decisions. Be honest with your agent. You should like and trust each other and work towards mutual goals. She should get to know and respect you. It is your job as an actor to also be a good businessperson.

Agent Carole R. Ingber of Ingber and Associates in New York says the relationship between actor and agent is like a marriage. When you're freelancing, it's like being engaged. You're getting to know each other and testing the relationship. If you find you both want to continue working together, you "get married," or sign a contract.

When looking for an agent, here are some issues you will want to consider:

- How big is the agent? Is there one particular agent who will work with you or is there an entire department of agents that you will need to maintain contact with? Do they have other divisions: theatre, film, television?
- How many of your type are already signed with her? How does the agent see your type?
- Do you feel the agent is eager to actively send you out? How often will she send you out, on the average?
- Does the agent have a good reputation among your actor friends and casting directors in your market? Is she honest? Trustworthy? Liked by other actors?
- If you sign, what is the length of the contract? Understand the union "out clause" and the union rules for agents. You may want to change agents or they may want to let you go.
- Do you get a good feeling from the agent and the way she does business? Do you trust her? Do you like her?

Remember, the agent wants to sign you because she believes in you—believes you can get jobs and she can make money as a result. If you don't make money, she doesn't make money. However, agents can only submit you. You have to win the jobs. It is still your responsibility to continue making contacts with casting directors and to tell them who your representation is. When my friend, Paula Plum, auditioned for a commercial agent in New York who agreed to freelance with her, the agent's parting words were, "Of course, you will continue to do your mailings to CDs."

CASTING DIRECTORS

How you work with casting directors depends entirely on the kind of system that has been established in your market. If you are working in an agent market, like Chicago, you will be called in by your agent. The casting directors do not want to be solicited by actors. It is the agent's job to send actors to the casting director. So in Chicago, it is not recommended to send your material to CDs. Your best and wisest route is through your agent.

Herb Mandell, a casting director in Orlando, likes to see new talent and even holds auditions once a week to get acquainted with who is out there. Then when calling the agent, he can ask for specific actors. Some CDs feel it saves them time to know the local talent pool and not just rely on the agent for that knowledge. It all depends on the system in your particular market.

Of course, if you are in a market where you are hired through casting directors, like Boston (non-agent or nonexclusive agent markets), you freelance through the agents and contact the casting directors directly.

What are your *responsibilities* in the partnership between you and the casting director or agent? Harrise Davidson, owner and talent agent of Davidson & Associates in Chicago, offers these words of wisdom: "Keep your skills up, perform in the theatre, keep your agent (or casting director) supplied with up-to-date pictures and resumes." If you don't keep pictures on file with your agent or CD, he cannot submit you for an audition. Also, always tell your agent when you are going to be out of town. If you do, the agent won't waste valuable time submitting you for jobs or trying to reach you when you're not available.

What are some actors' bad habits and things to avoid? Don't complain a lot. *Agents are your business partners, not your baby-sitters or therapists.* If you accept an audition and then cancel, don't complain if you are not getting work. If you are freelancing rather than signed, make sure you understand how often the agent wants you to check in. It's your job to stay in touch. And *always* show up early for an audition or job.

Maggie Trichon, owner and talent agent of Maggie, Inc., in Boston, suggests that you never drop in without an appointment. Make sure you look like your picture. Don't ask, "Why didn't you call me in for that audition?" or "Why aren't you calling me?" Don't personalize the rejection. Separate your ego from the business. And be professional and pleasant. Maggie says, "I love actors! But there are no guarantees."

Be professional, confident, pleasant, and look put together. And *don't lie!* Agents and casting directors want to feel good about submitting you.

DIRECTORS

How do you work with a director? What do directors look for in the casting session? If you ask Dan Driscoll, director and owner of September Productions in Boston, what qualities he looks for in an actor, he'll answer that he wants a range of interpretations and deliveries in the copy. This shows him the actor's creativity and skill. (Remember to prepare three different reads.)

Dan looks for an actor who is able to make changes. Some actors think they are making changes but often aren't. Being professional means having an endless number of acting choices at your disposal in a given moment, plus the skills to use them. After the director explains what he's looking for, the actor must be able to bring something to the party.

At some auditions, Dan asks the actor to do something totally off-the-wall to see what comes up. It may not be related at all to the copy. Always give it a shot. Never say, "I can't do that," unless it is a special skill you really can't do.

Bill Cuccinello, another director at September, also likes actors to explore, to try something totally new or different with the copy. He likes to do three different takes at the audition. On the first take, he gives the actor a brief outline of what he's looking for. On take two, he gives a lot of direction and sees how the actor uses it. And on the third take, Bill might ask for something totally different from the previous takes or build on something the actor has shown in a previous take.

Another quality directors look for is a pleasant personality. An actor should be fun to work with. However, Cuccinello points out that actors shouldn't try to entertain everybody on the set. That is not your job and can be distracting.

Perhaps the most difficult part about working with directors is that they do not always have a common language with actors. Many directors admit that they have not had any or enough acting training to help facilitate the communication process with actors or to understand how an actor's process works. Yet, most have learned from doing. And it is your job to come at least 80 percent of the way when directions are not clear. If you're unclear about a direction, reword it and ask if that's what he means. A good director will work with you and support you.

Acting in commercials is about results. You have to find the way to that result, the process, since you know it doesn't work to *play* a result. A director might say "Be more happy," or "Be funnier," or "Be more confused," or for a cold commercial, "Look sicker." Then it's your job to kick back to your "I want to . . .," and choose an action to play. This will give the director the result he's after.

(It's a good idea to have a whole range of symptoms for ailments and illnesses at your disposal for commercials. Every time you are sick, make a note about how you feel and where it hurts. It will be valuable in your future work.)

On the set, most directors want to make you as comfortable as possible with little or no tension. They want to make it easy for you to be creative. Yet there are those who scream and yell and intimidate people. It's very tough to know what to do in a situation like that other than protect yourself the best you can, do your work, and stay out of the way.

Directors, like everyone in this business, are under a lot of pressure. Commercials are created, developed, and executed by committee. They are made under the strictest deadlines and budgets and cost a fortune to produce. All participants, at every level of development, have their say. At the shoot, the whole show is on the director's shoulders. So appreciate his dilemma and help him out by being prepared and creative. Always stay on positive terms with the players on the production side.

(For a one-day shoot, the average cost to produce a regional commercial is between $30,000 and $125,000. The cost to produce a national spot in a one-day shoot will *start* at about $125,000.)

All directors agree that actors must do their homework. *You must show up prepared and have your lines thoroughly memorized, even though you may be asked to change them.* You are part of the creative process, which continually changes until the commercial is in the can.

Don't say you can do a special skill and then get hired for the job and get on the set and reveal that you really can't do it, like riding a horse or ice-skating or riding a motorcycle. This can cost the production company thousands of dollars in lost time and might very well be the end of your career. Really.

Remember, you are important and necessary. You may even feel *very* important since the camera is on you. Or you may feel you're out there all alone when the camera is rolling. But the bottom line is this: you are just one link in the whole process. Be prepared, confident, friendly, professional, and stay out of the way until you're needed—and you will be appreciated. You are there as one of many players in the process of making a successful commercial. You are there because they feel that you can do the job.

A Typical Day on the Job | 12

O nce you are booked for a commercial, you need to understand what is expected of you on the set. The production
company will move quickly from one setup to the next. It
is your job to be prepared and flexible at all times.

In advance of the day of the shoot, you should have all contract
issues confirmed.

Confirming the Contract

Part of your preparation is to *make sure you are clear on the details
of the job before you go to the location.* You or your agent should
know if you are a principal or extra, if the commercial is a regional
or national, if it is a dealer spot or demo or promotional, if you are
making one or more commercials, or if this commercial is to be cut
into more than one. You should know who the paymaster is. If you
don't have this basic information, call your agent, or if you are freelancing in a non-agent market, call the producer who booked you,
in advance. Also, know how many hours the day is planned to go
and add a couple of hours.

Don't be embarrassed to ask these questions. A good businessperson asks business questions. Any upstanding producer (in a
non-agent market) will be more than willing to answer. And the
person to ask is the producer, who has been hired by the client. It's
best to go to the source. (The casting director will likely be willing
to help also. But remember, the CD works for the client.) Or in an
agent market, ask your agent. It is the agent's job to get the contract nailed down.

Occasionally, you may run into someone who is trying to pull a fast one, such as not telling you the commercial will be cut into two spots, or saying you were an extra when you did principal work and were not upgraded to principal pay. A thorough knowledge of the job beforehand can help eliminate problems. Sometimes, however, these concerns surface on the set. Be aware of talk like "It's going to three markets. Let's do an alternate ending for Boston." When problems arise and you don't have an agent, call your union office for help. On nonunion jobs, the more details you can get up front the better protection you will have.

The Day Before the Shoot

A day or two before the actual shoot date, you may have a costume fitting, for which you are paid. The stylist or wardrobe person may request that you bring certain outfits of your own clothing, and she may also have brought other wardrobe selections for you to try. The wardrobe selections may need to be approved only by the stylist, or they may have to be approved by the director and/or client as well. It is possible that you will have your fitting on the day of the shoot.

If you have lines, request the copy and storyboard the day before the shoot, if it's possible to have them.

The Day of the Shoot

Here's how a typical schedule might look:

7:00 AM

Travel to the location. In most cities around the country, it is your responsibility to get to the location. However, in certain cities like New York, if the location is out of the city, the producer will arrange for your transportation. This may amount to picking up all the actors at a central place in Manhattan and driving you to the location on Long Island, for example. Or if you are traveling from one city to another, such as Manhattan to Orlando, the producer will arrange your travel.

If you are in most of the shots, your day will begin early. Commercials cost a fortune to make. Consequently, the company will want to shoot all your scenes in one day, if possible. If you're lucky, maybe you'll get two days' work.

8:00 AM

Arrive on the set at your specified call time with clean, set hair (for women), ready for the hair stylist. Bring any wardrobe that was requested. Always be a bit early.

Report to the assistant director (AD) or second assistant director (also AD) or production manager. This person may vary from shoot to shoot. But it is always easy to find them. Just say you are "talent" reporting in to the AD.

After you report in, *request any copy changes* and an updated storyboard from the AD.

Take your wardrobe to the wardrobe trailer or wardrobe room. Find the food setup, grab what you want, and head back to wardrobe and makeup. If your wardrobe has not yet been finalized, you will most likely report to wardrobe first, then to makeup. (If the shoot is in a building, the crew may set up a space there for these functions.) The wardrobe person may parade you past the director and client for final approval. They are looking at the character, not you. During makeup, study any new lines.

9:30 AM

When they are ready for you, you will be called to the set by the AD or assistant. You will do some run-throughs so the director can make technical adjustments to lighting, sound, props, and blocking. (If your action requires very specific or special moves, a grip or other technical person may work out your action with the director before you are called to the set.)

Here's an example. I did a shoot for the U.S. Postal Service where I played the owner of "Josie's" auto shop. In the first shot I am on an auto mechanic's dolly, lying on my back working under a car. My action is to zoom across the garage floor backwards on the dolly, change directions halfway across so I'm facing the doorway to the office, stop exactly in front of the door, pull myself up into the office (making it look easy and natural from lying flat on my back), wipe the grease from my hands, pick up the phone while pulling out my credit card, dial 1-800-STAMPS-24, and order stamps.

Before I got to the set, one of the grips practiced the moves with the camera so the director and camera person could see what kinds of problems would arise and what adjustments were needed. Because this was a very physical shot, it was wise of the director to rehearse this before calling me to the set. The grip passed on helpful hints about how to push off, how to turn the dolly, and how to land in front of the office doorway, and consequently we were able to get this complicated shot in about nine takes. This rehearsal technique also saved my energy for the other shots. (Any good director will save his actors' energy and not make you do all the technical rehearsals at full energy.) *Be conscious of conserving your energy.* Don't run around outside or use up unnecessary mental energy that you'll need for your takes.

Also, if you are doing a spokesperson or a dialogue, a smart director will suggest that you walk through the action for the first few rehearsals and save your "full acting" rehearsals for later, when all the technical problems are ironed out.

On any single shot, you may be asked to do anywhere between two and ninety takes. If everything and everybody is working well together it will be many fewer. But you never know. I was on a shoot once where the clients did not seem at all clear about what they wanted. (There were six of them in the next room watching each take on the monitor. This is very common. But the clients were also instructing the director about how to direct each and every take. This is not common.) I was waiting to be called for my shot. The actress before me was asked to do ninety takes of one line; yes, ninety! And she was a very good actress. I was just praying they would figure out what they wanted before I got out there. Fortunately, I ended up doing only twenty takes.

I did a shoot the other day, and we did three takes for each shot. I'd say we did about eight or nine sets of three, or twenty-four to twenty-seven takes total.

After your first shot is finished, they will reset camera, lighting, and location for the next shot.

In the interim, you will go to the trailer for any wardrobe changes and makeup touch-ups and to relax. Get something to drink or a snack if you need it. *Always be ready to return to the set in a moment.* The AD or assistant will come get you. They should never have to find you.

12:30 PM

Lunch. On union shoots you must be given between one-half and one hour for lunch. It is usually catered and pretty good. *Always bring something to wear over your costume when eating,* an old shirt or jacket. Or change clothes before eating. It's very important to protect your wardrobe, especially after it has been established in the previous shots.

Let the crew eat first. They were on the set one or two hours before you and have to go back to the set first.

1:30 PM

Head back to makeup for any touch-up or wardrobe changes. If it is clear that you are supposed to go right back to the set—for example, if you were in the middle of a shot before lunch—go to the set when you are ready. Otherwise wait to be called because, if they are resetting for a new shot, you will be in the way.

5:00 PM

In an ideal situation, you will be released after eight hours of work. Of course, sometimes you are released earlier, sometimes later. But the producer sticks to the schedule pretty closely, barring unforeseen difficulties, since time is money. If you work more than eight hours, not counting your lunch hour, you will be paid overtime.

If you had dialogue or lines, you may be asked to record "wild lines," which is extra audio-only recording of the actor's lines. This is done as a safety measure in case any of the sound recorded while the camera was rolling is not perfect.

Before you leave the set, say your thank-yous and good-byes. I specif-ically thank the director, cameraperson, the producer, any clients I have had contact with, and the crew. Just quick thank-yous. If you try to go back after you're out of wardrobe, many of the people will have left or the group will be too busy wrapping up or resetting for the next shot to talk.

After your work is finished, you will be released by the same person you have been dealing with all day, the AD or assistant. If you are there until the last shot, the director will say, "It's a wrap." The AD will give you a contract to sign. After the producer or AD has signed it, he will give you a copy. *Don't leave without a copy of your signed contract.*

Always be polite and friendly to everybody. Remember, you are just one spoke in a big wheel.

Leave any wardrobe and props in the trailer and be on your way.

5:30 TO 6:30 PM

Travel home.

Although the schedule will vary from job to job, this represents a typ-ical day on a commercial shoot.

Marketing Yourself or "The Business of the Business"

Y ou should not begin marketing yourself unless you can compete or already are competing on a professional level. For most actors and artists, self-marketing is one of the most difficult aspects of the business. There is a sense that as artists they should not have to be selling themselves. Actors also feel they don't have adequate skills to sell themselves. That's why we like to work with agents. It cuts down on the amount of self-marketing wc arc rcquircd to do. Some actors think that if they just send a picture and résumé once, they will be noticed and the casting director will know just how great they are—end of the marketing job. Well, it doesn't work that way. Getting seen, getting known, and marketing yourself consistently make up more than 50 percent of the work. It's like a series of ongoing job interviews. And if you don't do it, no one else will. If you don't get your face out there often, you won't get the agent or the jobs. Think of this as your own business. You are the product.

Once you are properly armed with all the tools of the trade, you're ready to get yourself out there in the marketplace, ready for hire. You should have theatre as well as on-camera training, a great picture and résumé, a reliable answering service or machine, a positive attitude, and plenty of energy and desire. If you start off half-prepared, you will be playing "catch-up" for a long time.

If you're already competing professionally but not getting the jobs, you need to rethink your "package" and tune it up to fit the needs of your market.

The most important marketing tools in the commercial acting business are

- *professional, classy products* (you, your picture and résumé, postcards, a demo tape of your commercial work)
- *a good answering service or machine*
- *a hunger to do the work*
- *long-term persistence,* and
- *a very positive attitude.*

Feeling confident about your skills and tools, let's take a look at getting started on your business marketing plan if you're in a market that has agents.

If You Work in a Market with Agents

All of the larger markets, like New York, Los Angeles, Chicago, and San Francisco, have agents. Whether you decide to freelance or sign with a given agency (in Los Angeles you must be signed), understand that the system is designed so that the jobs are available through agents. Therefore, your job is to get seen by them. How do you do that?

GATHERING INFORMATION

It is important to *design your business plan with a realistic strategy for implementing it.* Your best chance for some success in this highly volatile business is to get a realistic overview of your particular market, develop a plan of action, and begin the ongoing task of putting it into operation. Remember, the "business" of this business is like any other.

You want to consider all avenues of marketing such as direct mail, personal referral, theatre performances, SAG and AFTRA workshops, television, film and videos in which you are appearing, showcases, agents' and casting directors' workshops, seminars, and any other approaches you can discover.

TRADE PAPERS AND OTHER PUBLICATIONS

One of the best places to start gathering information is through the trade publications in one of the drama or theatre bookstores or at your union office. In New York, the first publication you will want to pick up is the *Ross Reports.* This journal is updated and published monthly. It is a guide to talent agents and personal managers nationwide and includes information such as the New York advertising agencies, talent agents, independent casting directors, television network studios, TV commercial producers, and much, much more. It provides a wealth of valuable information. For example, under the talent agents listings, it notes which agents are union signatories (those who are signed to and abide by the actors' union contracts), which ones attend theatrical showcase productions, which ones have facilities for viewing or listening to your video or audiotapes, and so on. It also specifies whether agents accept pictures and résumés, phone calls, or visits.

Ross Reports is available in single copies at bookstores, outlets, and some union offices, or through its publisher: Television Index, Inc., 40-29 Twenty-seventh Street, Long Island City, New York 11101 (708/937-3990).

In Los Angeles there is a book called *The Agencies,* which is updated and published every month and provides similar information to that in the *Ross Reports* for the West Coast. It lists the names, addresses, phone numbers, and other details about all the Los Angeles talent agents and subagents, as well as the types and levels of clients they represent (for example, new talent, nonunion talent, children, adults only, character actors and actresses, voice-over talent, commercials, equity, film, stars, literary). In addition, *The Agencies* gives evaluations of the agents listed and their reputations, such as "respected," "hardworking," "long established," "experienced." The editors also report any questionable practice by unlicensed or unfranchised agents and give good advice to actors about how to protect themselves in this business. *The Agencies* is published by Acting World Books, P.O. Box 3044, Hollywood, CA 90078. *LA Agent Book,* by K Callan, gives a brief synopsis of each agent, what they do, and how many clients they have. Callan also has a book on New York agents.

Another excellent publication, *CD Directory,* is published by Breakdown Services for both the Los Angeles and New York markets. The directory is a comprehensive listing of casting directors in each market. In the Los Angeles version, casting directors are listed both geographically and alphabetically. Commercial casting facilities are also listed. Another plus is the listing of the casting directors' assignments for the current year's television season. The directory is published every three months and updated every two weeks. For an annual subscription to the LA *CD Directory,* call 310/276-9166. For the NY *CD Directory,* call 212/869-2003. Each is approximately $40 for the year. In addition, Breakdown Services sells labels for casting directors, and commercial and SAG agents for both the New York and Los Angeles markets.

Most trade papers and other publications worth investigating can be found in the performing arts bookstore in your market. Or browse through the "film" and "theatre arts" sections of any good bookstore. The Drama Bookstore in New York, for example, has mailing label lists for each of the major categories of work, including lists of commercial agents. You may want to start by mailing only to those agents looking for new talent. As you gather information for marketing and plan your strategy, keep in mind that you will be marketing yourself for as long as you stay in the business. That could be ten, fifteen, or twenty-five years. Also *think about your follow-through plan for at least a year in advance.* For example, if you are planning to do a major mailing of, say, two hundred pictures and résumés, would it be cost and time effective to buy a mailing label list rather than hand-type or write out all the agents' names and addresses yourself *each time?* Or could you buy these labels and xerox them onto other labels for a second mailing down the road? Do the labels you're considering fit on your postcards as well? What about follow-up? After the mailing of your headshot and résumé, when and how often will you follow up with a postcard? In New York, actors send postcards once a month; in the smaller markets, less often. Since persistence is such a large factor in the business, plan your follow-up and stick with it. These are the issues you need to consider in planning your marketing strategy.

While you're in the bookstore, pick up any weekly or monthly magazines and newspapers about the business and browse through them. In New York there is *Back Stage,* which is a performing arts weekly newspaper. It has information and services, articles and columns, about all areas of the performing arts, including plenty of national and regional information. You can find places to have your résumé formatted and copied, ads for headshot photographers, mailing services who will do your bulk mailings for you, classes and lessons in all aspects of acting, general theatre auditions in the area, both union and nonunion, news about SAG, AFTRA, and Equity contracts, ads for answering services, psychotherapy groups for performers—you name it. Other trade papers that provide valuable information on what is playing and being produced, upcoming productions in theatre, film, and television, and the "business of the business" include *Variety, The Hollywood Reporter, Hollywood Variety, Drama-logue,* and *Back Stage West,* and are all available in industry bookstores and on the newsstands in major theatre districts. Most medium- to larger-size markets have publications that cover these issues for the performing arts.

Since it pays to "know the business," national and regional editions of trade publications for the advertising industry, such as *Advertising Age* and *AdWeek,* are worth reading. They will tell you which ad agencies have which accounts—those commercials you audition for. Part of your strategy may be to market yourself directly to the commercial divisions of ad agencies, particularly if they have in-house casting directors.

Forms of Self-Marketing

Once you've gathered all your information, you need to decide which approaches you will employ: direct mail, personal referral, showcases, agents' workshops, and so forth.

DIRECT MAIL

Direct mail consists of a mass mailing of your picture and résumé with a short note to agents and casting directors. It is widely used as a major form of marketing in most markets. Naturally, your mailing should look very professional. Here are some things to consider. Do you want to have some consistency in the total look of your mailing? For example, if you have your résumé done on a good-quality ivory paper, it might be a good idea to send your short note on the same paper. Or maybe the paper should be note-sized rather than the same size as your résumé. Do you handwrite or type the note? Should you also use ivory mailers to maintain the theme? Should you have your own mailing labels made up with your name logo on them? Should you carry out this name logo theme on your résumé and notepaper?

Remember, *as long as what you do is classy and professional,* anything you can do that stands out from everybody else is a benefit. You do *not* want to send your résumé on hot-pink or electric-green paper. Shock value is not what we're after here. If you decide to have your stationery customized, for both your résumé and notepaper, you'd better love it for two reasons: it costs money, and you'll need to use it for quite some time.

As part of your direct mail plan, let's say you're sending out head-shots and résumés with a note. What should your note say? Keep it to three or four sentences, something like this:

(For agents who accept calls:)

Dear _____,

I just played [character] in [play] at [theatre] and am now auditioning for commercials. I would appreciate the opportunity to audition for you. I'll call you the week of March 6 to set up an appointment. Thanks for your consideration.

(Or for agents who do not accept calls:)

Dear _____,

I just completed a class in commercials with _____. I'm freelancing through [list agents' names] and would like to work with you, too. Thanks for keeping me in mind.

(Or if you're an established actor who has just relocated:)

Dear _____,

I've just arrived in New York from Boston, where I made my living in the-atre and commercials. _____, the casting director, suggested I contact you. I am enclosing my short commercial reel of both national and regional spots. I'll give you a call in two weeks to arrange to audition for you. Thanks for watching.

You get the idea. Use your own words. Take what you consider your strongest points that would appeal to the agent or casting director and present them in a warm, inviting, businesslike way. Remember, never lie. And keep it short. Always *think the way the agent thinks.* Evaluate it. Be tough. How would you react if you just received this mailing? How can you improve it?

Always call to confirm the spelling of the person's name to whom you're writing, and the address. Also, make sure the person is still there. If not, ask where she's moved to and follow up. People change jobs quite often in agencies.

FOLLOW-UP

In your planning, decide beforehand how you intend to follow up. If you do a two-hundred-piece mailing and intend to follow up by phone with all two hundred pieces in two weeks, you're a better person than I am. First of all, many agents do not accept calls, so that kills that idea. But for those who do accept calls, make sure you do call or visit them when you say you will. It's pretty ambitious to reach ten agents or casting directors by phone in a week's time. You might stagger your mailing and your follow-up, mailing twenty pieces each week for two months, for example.

Let's assume you have done a two-hundred-piece mailing and most of the agents say, "Do not call or visit." Now what? Postcard mailings are an excellent way to stay in touch. Be sure your name is on the front, as well as SAG, AFTRA, and AEA (Actor's Equity Association, the stage actors' union) if you are a member. In the larger markets, actors are reluctant to have their home phone numbers printed on the card, so list their service number. Mail the information in an envelope if you prefer. Be sure your service, machine number, or current agent's number, if not printed somewhere in the mailing, is written in your message; otherwise the agent or casting director will never be able to find you. With no phone number, the postcard or note goes into the trash. No one should have to work to find you.

The postcard follow-up should be the same shot as your headshot. Through repeat advertising, so to speak, you want people to start to get your name and face in their minds. Sometimes actors use two different shots on their postcards to show their diversity: a casual mom and a professional businesswoman, for example. This is worth considering if you look very different in each shot, including hair, wardrobe, and point of view; and a good idea if you are working in more than just the commercial market, which most actors do.

Many actors do postcard mailings once a month. That's twelve times a year. Big job. But if you're serious about the business, it may take just this kind of effort. Others do mailings four to six times a year. It depends on your overall plan and your geographic market. In the beginning, when you're trying to get noticed for the first time, you may want to do more. It's best if you have some progress to report in those mailings, like "I just did a showcase for so-and-so," or "I just did a commercial class with so-and-so," or "I was just put on hold for a Pampers national spot." Anything you can report that shows you are busy and making progress. *Always* keep it short. Think the way the agent would when receiving these postcards and remember that in the largest markets they receive hundreds of these a week.

PERSONAL REFERRAL

If you're already established in the business, have been freelancing through several agents, or your contract is up with your current agent and you're looking to sign with another, your marketing plan will be different. In this case, of course, the best of all worlds is to be personally introduced to an agent through a casting director or an actor friend who is already signed with that agent.

Nothing works better than personal referral. Nothing. Of course, personal referral does not guarantee you'll get that agent or job. But who you know is definitely a big plus.

From the time you entered the business, you've probably met lots of people. Call in your favorites. Think of anyone who could help you get a personal introduction at any of the agencies you're interested in. At this point in your career, you might be interested in getting in with one particular agent. I hope you research the agencies enough to know which one or ones will work for you. I have a friend in New York who was quite happy freelancing through several smaller agents simultaneously but who felt she would be better off signing with one larger agency. So after implementing a variety of direct mail marketing efforts and after a couple of personal referrals, she was offered to sign with one the biggest agencies. Now she finds that, because the agency is so large, and because she ends up having to work with four or five of the commercial agents within that one agency, she gets lost in the shuffle. She preferred freelancing through several of the smaller or medium-sized agencies because she was able to develop personal relationships with specific agents at each of those agencies. Of course, that has to be traded off with this economy and the uncertain times. Agents call their signed actors before using freelance actors. And signing with a big agency offers a certain amount of prestige. It's all a balancing act, which has to be analyzed and adjusted on a regular basis according to your needs, your type, the economy, your geographic market, the amount of available work in your market, and other factors.

I have a friend in Los Angeles who has been in the business for twenty years. He does it all: commercials, TV series, movies, theatre. He has always played good supporting roles. But he wanted to try to get into the leading-man roles. He was getting bored with the same types of supporting roles; they all seemed like the same character, only with a different name. So he decided that after working for ten years with the same legit agent and not getting sent up for the kind of leading roles he was interested in playing, he would change agents. Now, here's a guy who has been a working actor for twenty years. Makes a very nice living. You'd think he would have no problems switching agents with his credits and history. Right? Wrong. He couldn't get another agent for almost a year. Why? Part of it was that he left one agent before researching and getting another agent; part of it was his type (maybe the guy would not be cast as anything other than a supporting character); part of it was his age; part of it was the economy; part of it was the number of actors of his type in his market; and part of it he'll never figure out since you rarely get feedback. So even for established actors, a well-planned, ongoing marketing strategy is vital.

I used to think that once I got established I wouldn't have to continue marketing myself. After fifteen years of making my living in the business, I figured everybody knew me and I didn't have to keep getting their attention. Not so. Sure, there are those times when you are the right type, have the right skills, are the right age, right color, right sex, have the right color of hair, and you get really busy for a year or two. Those who are lucky enough to make their living in the business all have about five minutes of fame. But eventually, you get too old, or overexposed, or the market changes, or the type they want changes, or you're a woman over forty or a minority of any age, or all your contacts leave the business and a new generation of agents and directors arrive and your five minutes are up.

The point is you have to *adapt to the times and keep your marketing plan and career innovative and diversified.* The more areas of the acting industry you can work in, including commercials, theatre, television, film, training films, print, and teaching, the better your chances of longevity.

Other Self-Marketing Ideas

What about other ideas for long-term direct mail marketing? Anything you can think of that's catchy, classy, and professional might work. Cute and eye-catching material alone isn't sufficient, however. Whatever you send out should have a businesslike message and should tell of work you've recently done. I have written short poems and attached clever Post-it notes that say things like "Thanks for thinking of me," with recent jobs listed. One time I did a mailing on my computer with a Symbol typeface that looks like Greek. I sent it to all the casting directors, freelance directors, and producers and directors in production companies.

In Athens they say:

ΔΟΥΓΑΝ ΔΕΦΙΝΙΤΕΛΨ ΔΕΛΙςΕΡΣ

In Boston they say:

DOUGAN DEFINITELY DELIVERS!

INDUSTRIALS	COMMERCIALS
SPOKESPERSON	CHARACTERS
TRADE SHOWS	VOICEOVERS
EAR PROMPTER	PRINT

Any holiday, special occasion, president's birthday, plus job news can be a good reason to do a clever mailing. If you are on a shoot, it's a good idea to take a camera and have the lighting- or cameraperson snap a picture of you in action, especially if you are doing principal work with any stars. Then have postcards of that shot made up, and do a mailing. But never impose on the stars or crew or interfere with the shooting schedule. You need to feel this out before you decide to try it. Use good common sense. Don't hurt the image of actors by being one of "those" actors.

I did a promo once for NBC for their new fall television series. I worked with several of their prime-time stars. Our cameraman and director took pictures of the whole group, and I had postcards made showing me with various stars. Then I did mailings. As a marketing tool, that worked well for me for a couple of years. Always keep it professional with a note about your work.

THEATRE PRODUCTIONS AND SHOWCASES

Theatrical showcases and theatre productions are another good approach. In fact, most good agents won't take you on until they've seen your work, either live or on film. Can you blame them? Wouldn't you be curious if you signed before the agent saw your work?

When you are appearing in a showcase or play, do a mailing to all the agents who note that they attend productions. In fact, you may need to do more than one mailing over the course of several weeks before the performance. I find that it takes three "hits" before the agent or director takes notice. And when they are getting hundreds of similar materials from other actors, *methodical* persistence on your part is definitely a must. You cannot be assured that any agents will attend, even given all the effort you've put into your marketing. All you can do is try to get them there, and eventually someone will attend. (Be sure to offer complimentary tickets to all who can hire you. Since the theatre producers will limit your comps, ask about professional comps and/or be prepared to pay for additional comps.) I have friends who have gotten commercial agents through theatrical showcases. Agents like to know that you're a "real actor" for all areas of work.

CLASSES, SEMINARS, AND WORKSHOPS

Agents and casting directors often are asked to teach seminars, workshops, and classes for actors on all kinds of topics. This is a great way to be seen. However, there is often a condition stated in the class registration material specifying that the casting director or agent is not allowed to cast anyone who takes the class for a certain length of time after the conclusion of the class. Or a class brochure will specifically state that by taking the class you are not in any way guaranteed employment or auditions. That's OK. If you think a particular agent or casting director is worth working with in a seminar, it might help you get noticed.

A Caution

A note of caution. I'm sorry to say that in all major markets there are people who are out to make a dollar off of actors without providing a good service. Any time you are considering taking a workshop or class or getting involved in a "network" that says it is a liaison to agents or makes promises of employment, ask for names of three previous students. Agents are not allowed to run acting schools, either. They can't force you to take specific classes or workshops or use a particular photographer. If you are a victim of foul play or are being pressured by any agent or agent's liaison, protect yourself by calling your union office or your state licensing board to see if these people are aboveboard professionals, and what one of them can and cannot legally do as an agent or liaison. It's a tough enough business, and you don't want to waste your time and money on a class or service that will get you nothing but angry. Be smart and investigate these things before signing up.

The Unions

Another good way to get information is through the two acting unions, Screen Actors Guild and the American Federation of Television and Radio Artists. If you live in one of the medium or larger markets, you will have a local union office. You must be a member to attend workshops or get a list of the signatories in your area. Many of the union workshops are designed to help you develop or improve your marketing approach to the business by having guests in the business like agents, casting directors, or others give talks telling how they want to be pursued.

By all means talk to your actor friends who are working in your market. They are often the absolutely best source of current information about what's happening and how to make contacts since they are doing it. Take an actor out to lunch. They usually love to commiserate and talk about what they're doing.

If You Work in a Market Without Agents

If you are working in a market where there are no agents, chances are the job opportunities will be available through independent casting agents, production companies, and sometimes even through the clients themselves. Find out who the casting directors are through the yellow pages of your phone book or through any local publications about the business.

The approach to investigating your particular market may seem a little bit less clear than in major cities since you probably won't have the benefit of a publication like the *Ross Reports* or *The Agencies.* However, there is always a way to find out what's going on and whom to contact to get the auditions and jobs.

Casting Directors and Producers In a non-agent market you need to find out who takes the place of the agent. The bottom line is: how do actors get hired for commercials in a non-agent market? Most often the hiring is through independent casting agents (who work for the client), in-house ad agency casting directors and/or producers, and producers at commercial production houses.

Signatory List One of the first things to do in a non-agent market is to get a list of the signatories from your local SAG or AFTRA office. These are the production companies, casting directors, ad agencies, and clients who have signed an agreement to abide by the union contracts and hire only union talent. If you are not a union member or do not have a local union office, do not despair. There are plenty of ways to get information.

Bookstores Again, find a drama bookstore or the bookstore where you would purchase plays and related materials. If any publications are available, you will find them here. These bookstores will also carry any acting-related newspapers that list casting notices, classes, seminars, teachers, coaches, and so on.

Actors' Organizations In some cities, there are actor organizations or resource centers. Boston, for example, has an organization called Stage-Source, The Alliance of Theatre Artists and Producers. It is a resource center for actors, directors, administrators, technicians, producers, and audience members. Member benefits include listings in the casting files, casting, job and discount-ticket hot lines, a bimonthly newsletter, professional workshops and seminars, and the best annual theatre party in Boston. StageSource also puts out a publication called *The Source* every two years, which is considered the actor's bible to New England. It lists talent, print, and modeling agencies; film, video, and audio producers; all theatre companies, both union and nonunion; ad agencies; teachers; schools; and professional services and supplies. It also contains articles on how to get a great headshot and résumé, how to produce an audio and video demo tape, how to use an ear prompter, and on and on.

Scout around your market to find any similar resource groups. Or start your own. StageSource was started by theatre professionals. It has three staffers and operates with volunteers.

Other Actors Look for ways to make contact with other actors who are already working in your market. Through SAG and AFTRA seminars and workshops or membership meetings, you can get to know some other actors and share information and resources. Don't, however, expect other actors to share the names of their contacts. Some will be willing to do this and some won't. It depends on your market and the amount of competition. Actors work hard to get contacts, so don't expect these names to be handed to you. You will have to work for them, too.

The Yellow Pages For another source of contacts, your local telephone book yellow pages is a great source. Look under video or commercial production and ad agencies. When you call, ask if they have a casting director or maintain casting files; then send your package to a specific person.

GROUP MARKETING

If you are a nonunion actor and have no union, resource center, or group support, consider starting a group. If you know absolutely no one in your city, you can always put an ad in the actors' newspaper and say that you'd like to start a commercial actors' support group to share information and ideas, or an actors' marketing group.

One good reason to start a group for self-marketing is to share the time, contacts, and expense of the effort. Of course, you have to have something in common; for example, AEA, SAG, and AFTRA membership. A professional group of actors may carry some status with casting directors and agents. If the group is in all three unions, it establishes that you all have paid your dues and worked hard to become professionals. Or perhaps you have a theatre group together.

The point is you want the producers, directors, or casting directors who receive your group marketing materials to say, "Gee, that's a clever idea. Maybe I could see the whole group at once and save some time"— not "Why are they sending me this mailing as a group?"

Think about the casting director's point of view. Would your group marketing benefit the casting directors? Maybe it would and maybe it wouldn't. You'll need to decide for yourself and your market. Instead of group marketing, you may decide for everyone in your group to share his individual contacts, work in a joint effort on the labels, and then market himself individually.

How To Make Contact

Once you have established a list of the companies, agencies, and production houses, the next step is to make contact with them. Call each of them. Ask if they do commercial productions, if they maintain casting files, and ask for the name and title of the person to whom you should send your materials. You should also ask what materials they accept: pictures, résumés, video demo reels? Do they prefer VHS or 3/4-inch format; and for voice-over demo tapes, cassette or reel-to-reel?

Always send your material to a specific person—the producer, casting director, director, or person who maintains the casting files. Otherwise your material will end up in the trash. Remember to update your files every time you do a mailing. Personnel changes a lot in this business, so you want to make sure you're sending your stuff to the correct person. If your contact has moved, ask to what agency, so you can maintain contact.

Getting your contact list together takes a lot of phone time. You may have to speak to three or four departments in a given agency or company before you get to the right person. Be patient and be pleasant. Don't try to do it all in one day. Decide how much time you can spend on it each week. Part of your marketing plan must be a realistic execution of that plan.

Realistically, it can take you several months to complete your first round of mailings and follow-ups, especially since most actors have to make some money while they're getting and keeping themselves established. That's OK. Presumably you're in this for the long haul. All your marketing work is just like starting and maintaining your own business. Self-marketing is a key aspect of this business and must be done on a regular basis. It's all part of being a professional actor.

Other Marketing Ideas

Although direct mail with phone follow-up is a primary method of marketing yourself, there are other things you can do, too. You might consider joining one of the local branches of a producer/director organization like ITVA, International Television and Video Association. They hold local meetings, seminars, and workshops as well as national conventions. It's a good place to network and meet producers and directors.

You may want to consider taking out an ad in one of the publications for directors and/or producers in your market. There are tons of ideas for self-marketing. You are limited only by your imagination. I've seen a postcard with pictures of actors who are married to each other. On the left half they appear in business clothes with a serious point of view and on the right half they are total characters, like a bag lady and a nerd. Under the pictures they list the types of work they do, like commercials, characters, voice-overs. The postcard was reproduced well and got them a lot of notice and work. Another acting couple I know do up Christmas cards with pictures of themselves trimming the tree and each other.

I've seen other ideas straight out of one of those product marketing catalogues, like pencils with slogans printed on them incorporating the actor's name, wallet-sized calendars, and tip cards with the actor's picture on the back. You can use Easter to send "egg" or "bunny" pictures. I've seen postcards designed to show the name or theme of the play in which the actor was appearing. You can do anything as long as it has class with a sense of humor. But whatever the occasion, *the message of these mailings should be business-related, reporting progress in your work.*

Many actors now carry a business card with their picture on it. Many of the self-marketing ideas beginning on page 116 can apply here, too.

Keeping Records of Your Contacts

Keep a record of all your contacts. I use two small three-ring binders that list alphabetically all my contacts, marketing efforts, auditions, and jobs with every company. Sometimes you will have several contacts at a company, sometimes just one person. I write down things like when someone goes on vacation, having gleaned this from a phone conversation; if he bought a house, had a kid, got married; what jobs I worked on with him; what I said on the postcard I sent; when I sent a new headshot and résumé; what agency he moved to when he left this one; the whole ball of wax. With so many contacts, it's critical to keep track of these things and fun to look back at your notes after many years.

Of course, you could do this on a computer, too. I have a friend who has a pocket computer. At every audition or job, he enters the names, addresses, and phone numbers of his contacts right there. Some people may do it on index cards at home after the job or audition. It doesn't really matter what form you use for your records, as long as they're organized and easy to access and update. Recording this information also helps you keep track of the number of auditions versus the number of jobs won in any given period.

Keep in mind that your self-marketing strategy requires short- and long-term planning, repeated execution, and plenty of persistence. It can actually be fun and creative much of the time, and tedious some of the time, too. It's a fact of life in the business, a mandatory component of professional acting. So you may as well learn to enjoy it.

The Unions | *14*

Most professional actors become union members. There are three primary actors' unions: Screen Actors Guild (SAG), the American Federation of Television and Radio Artists (ATFRA), and Actors Equity Association (AEA), which is the stage actors' union. Two "sister unions" are the American Guild of Variety Artists (AGVA) and the American Guild of Musical Artists (AGMA).

Most actors who work on-camera are members of SAG and AFTRA. In 1992, SAG had 88,848 members nationally and AFTRA had a national membership of about 75,000.

SAG's jurisdiction includes performers who work in film: movies, filmed TV shows, filmed commercials, corporate and educational films, student and experimental films, and music videos.

AFTRA represents performers, including newscasters and announcers. AFTRA's jurisdiction includes anything that is produced live or on tape: videotape, audiotape, phonograph recordings, radio, and live television.

Both AFTRA and SAG are national organizations with many local or branch offices around the country.

Benefits

SAG and AFTRA negotiate and enforce contracts to guarantee wages and working conditions for their members.

There are many benefits in joining one or both of these professional unions. As stated on the SAG and AFTRA membership information sheets, these benefits include:

- Professional status.
- A guaranteed minimum wage paid on time.
- Guaranteed payment for overtime, residuals, travel time, and the like.
- Safe and proper working conditions.
- Grievance and arbitration procedures.
- Medical, dental, and pension benefits once you earn a required amount.
- Eligibility for membership in the AFTRA/SAG Federal Credit Union in Los Angeles.
- Eligibility to apply for major credit cards at reduced interest rates.

Many local branch offices around the country also have a variety of other services, which may include casting/job hot lines, newsletters, member talent guides for producers, workshops, and seminars.

But remember, membership does not guarantee work. *Neither of these unions secures work for any of its members. But they make sure the work you get is secure.*

Your Responsibilities

Both SAG and AFTRA have what is known as Rule One. It requires that members work only for companies who have signed each union's collective bargaining agreements. These companies are called signatories.

In order to keep the union strong and its members protected, it is your responsibility to abide by all the rules and regulations. Members are required (as noted, again, on the SAG and AFTRA membership information sheets) to:

- Be professionally prepared for each job (know your lines, come with clean and neat hair, face, and correct wardrobe).
- Arrive early.
- Bring a contract to every job, even though the producers usually provide one. Leave every job with a signed contract.
- Pay your dues on time.
- Attend meetings.
- Vote.
- Report any violations or problems to your local office.
- Get involved. It's your union!

Initiation Fees and Dues

The price to join each of the actors' unions is high. But when you consider what you make for each job and the benefits you get as a result, the cost seems small. As of July 1993, SAG costs $1,012.50 ($970 initiation fee plus first semiannual basic dues of $42.50) to join. AFTRA's initiation fee is determined by each local branch and is in the range of $600 to $800 plus $42.50 minimum semiannual dues. Annual dues for both unions are on a sliding scale and are determined by the amount you earned the previous year.

How Can I Join?

You can walk into an AFTRA office, plunk down your money, and become a member without any eligibility requirement. To join SAG, however, you must have done at least one day of principal work or three days of extra work; or else you must be a member of one of the sister unions (listed on page 127) for one year and you must have done principal work under that union's jurisdiction.

When Should I Join?

You have no business joining any union unless you are ready to make a commitment to the profession. As you know, you will be competing with the best in the field who are already working. It will become clear to you when you should join. You will feel confident in your work, get good feedback by booking jobs, and/or you will win a job and be given a SAG or AFTRA contract.

A colleague and I were participating in a panel at a regional theater on "How to Make a Living as an Actor," when someone asked her about joining SAG and AFTRA. She said, "Deciding to join the unions is a lifetime commitment." That's a very appropriate way to put it. Joining should not be a casual decision. There are too many members and too much competition as it is. You must be professionally trained, properly motivated, and have the money. Can you imagine joining the union prematurely and never getting work again because you can't compete?

Nonunion Work

Your goal before joining a union is to gain on-the-job experience in the nonunion market. One of the benefits of being nonunion is that in these tough economic times, producers are looking for more nonunion talent since it costs them less. There are even professionals who only work nonunion, by choice, since in some markets there either is little or no union work. Nonunion does not necessarily mean nonprofessional.

The drawbacks to nonunion work are that you do not have the protection of the union when you can't collect your pay or when you are having trouble negotiating a decent rate of pay. You do not have the union's protection when it comes to safe working conditions or the number of hours you work. You also get no residuals or overtime, unless you negotiate it. You get no benefits, no health or dental insurance, or pension plan. And you only have yourself to enforce any agreement. You don't have the union.

If you are working nonunion, make sure you get a clear understanding before the job begins about work hours, rate of pay, when you will be paid, by whom, and any other questions.

What Will I Be Paid For a Sag or Aftra Commercial?

Generally, under a SAG or AFTRA contract for a wild spot (a commercial that is contracted to air on a station-by-station basis, rather than on a network), as an on-camera principal you will be paid $414.25 for the basic session fee. This is one eight-hour day. This rate *excludes* New York, Los Angeles, and Chicago, where rates are higher. For this fee, the client is allowed use of the commercial for a thirteen-week period. If it runs for more than thirteen weeks, you will be paid residuals. You could be paid additional money based on *where it airs* (which and how many markets) and *how it's broadcast* (local stations versus a network, for example). All of your earnings will have federal taxes, social security, Medicare, and state taxes withheld.

This gives you a rough idea of what you can make for a day's work. But remember that you will not be working every day. Far from it. For the realities of making a living in the business, please read Chapter 15: Can I Really Make a Living?

Remember, **if you are a union member, you may not work nonunion.** You would weaken every union member's security as well as the union's bargaining position with producers. If you want to work nonunion, do not join the unions. You cannot have it both ways. I know two union members who worked nonunion jobs and were reported. One was fined a large sum of money, and the other had to get up in front of the entire local membership and give an apology.

Once you join one union, you may not work any nonunion job on audiotape, videotape, or film. As a member of one of the sister unions such as SAG or AFTRA, you might be allowed to work in a nonunion theatre under a "guest artist" contract or for a university theatre with a URTA contract (University Resident Theatre Association) *if* the contract is granted to you by Actors' Equity Association. It is your responsibility to check with your union before considering any employment at a nonunion theatre.

If you're not prepared to make the commitment—professionally, financially, and for the long haul—don't join the unions.

Can I Really Make a Living? | *15*

ood question. There are a variety of factors you need to look at to draw your own conclusions. They are

- Actual earnings data
- Diversity of work
- Markets where the work is available
- Readiness to compete professionally
- Age, gender, and ethnicity
- Whom you know, luck
- And really wanting it.

Let's assume you are competing professionally or are prepared to do so. You have some contacts, you're feeling lucky, and you really, really want this life more than anything else. With these benefits on your side, let's look at the hard-core facts of the business.

Actual Earnings

Figure 15–1 provides a range of data including SAG earnings under all contracts and membership data for the years 1982, 1989, 1990, 1991, and 1992. Look at the figures and compare them from year to year.

```
1982
        52,000    SAG members

         $8,827   Approximate average earnings (all members)
         40,000   Members earning less than $1,000        (77%)
         42,120   Members earning less than $5,000        (81%)
          1,841   Members earning $50,000 or more          (3.54%)

    $459,000,000  Total earnings under all contracts:

 (more than 50%) Earnings under Commercials Contract
          (35%)  Earnings under Television Contract
          (12%)  Earnings under Theatrical Contract
  (less than 1%) Earnings under Industrial/Educational Contract

            46%  Members living in LA                    (23,920)
            36%  Members living in NY                    (18,720)
            18%  Members living outside NY or LA          (9,360)

1989
         76,502  Active SAG members

        $12,013  Average annual earnings (all members)
         $8,895  Average earnings - women
        $14,324  ' Average earnings - men
         22,702  Members with zero earnings              (30%)

    $940,000,000 Total earnings under all contracts:

         20,213  Total on-camera principal roles under Commercials
                 Contract:
                 women - 8,359 roles
                 men - 11,854 roles
          9,440  Total roles in Feature Films:
                 women - 2,747 roles
                 men - 6,693 roles
         39,161  Total roles in Television:
                 women - 13,863 roles
                 men - 25,298 roles

1990
         81,000  SAG members

        $12,596  Approximate average earnings (all members)
          8,100  Approximate number of members earning $25,000
                 or more                                 (10%)
```

Figure 15-1: Screen Actors Guild data. Sources: "The Female In Focus: In Whose Image?" Screen Actors Guild, August 1990; *Screen Actor Magazine,* Fall 1990; "Employment In Entertainment: The Search for Diversity," Screen Actors Guild, June 1993; Robert Cain, Director of Research, SAG-Hollywood, 1993; Douglass Bergmann, Director of Research, SAG-Hollywood, 1994; SAG Membership Department Records, Hollywood, 1994

2,261	Members earning more than $100,000 (2.791%)
$1,021,000,000	Total earnings under all contracts (more than twice the amount in 1982)
36%	Earnings under Commercials Contract
38%	Earnings under Television Contract
25%	Earnings under Theatrical Contract
1%	Earnings under Industrial/Educational Contract
21%	Approximate number of members living outside of NY or LA (17,000)

1991

84,000	SAG members
$11,920	Approximate average earnings (all members) (5.3% less than 1990)
2,144	Members earning more than $100,000 (2.55%)
$1,000,000,000	Total earnings under all contracts ($21 million less than 1990):
38%	Earnings under Commercials Contract
36%	Earnings under Television Contract
24%	Earnings under Theatrical Contract
Less than 1%	Earnings under Industrial/Educational Contract

1992

88,848	SAG members	
$11,281	Average earnings (all members)	
$10,871	Average earnings - women	
$14,138	Average earnings - men	
35,379	Members earning $3,000 or less	(39.8%)
2,098	Members earning more than $100,000	(2.4%)
$1,002,292,738	Total earnings under all contracts (increase of 3.8% or $2.3 million more than 1991):	
38%	Earnings under Commercials Contract	$380,765,338
39.1%	Earnings under Television Contract	$391,770,076
22%	Earnings under Theatrical Contract	$220,518,423
9%	Earnings under Industrial/Educational Contract	$9,238,901

Since these figures are compiled from a wide range of sources, all data is approximate.

Reprinted by permission of the Screen Actors Guild.

Figure 15-1 Screen Actors Guild data, continued

What conclusions can we draw from these figures? The good news is that although TV programs and films occasionally exceed commercial earnings, *in any given year total earnings in commercials are usually the highest.* In numbers of jobs, during 1992 alone, there were approximately 77,500 on-camera principal roles in TV commercials and 53,500 TV commercial voice-over jobs (according to Roger Lateiner, head of research at SAG in New York).

The bad news is that the average earnings of SAG members under all contracts do not appear to be increasing. In fact, they have crept down to $11,281 in 1992 from $12,569 in 1990. Also, *large numbers of members earn very little money in any given year.* For example, in 1982, 40,000 members earned less than $1,000. Ten years later, in 1992, about 35,379 members earned $3,000 or less. (When adjusted for inflation, that $3,000 figure is only an improvement of between $900 and $1,200 over 1982, rather than what appears to be an increase of $2,000.)

Most people can't live on these average earnings. And keep in mind that the number of SAG members increases each year. Many members earn additional income under AFTRA and Equity contracts, however.

Comparable AFTRA earnings figures are not available. At this writing, AFTRA's computer system cannot access divisions of earnings of this kind, since many of their members are not freelance but employed by television stations. According to Fred Wilhelms of AFTRA Health and Retirement in New York, in 1990 AFTRA members earned just over $25 million under the TV commercials contract, compared to $367,560,000 for SAG members under their commercials contract. Since most television commercials are made on film rather than videotape and hence fall under the jurisdiction of SAG, this accounts for the much smaller earnings figures under the AFTRA TV commercials contract.

Diversity of Work

There are some actors in New York and Los Angeles who work exclusively in television commercials, but the majority of professional actors work under as many contracts as possible, since this helps to increase their total income. If in your geographic market you can do television commercials, television programs, theatrical films (movies), industrial and educational videos and films, and voice-overs, your chance of making a living exclusively from acting may improve somewhat. (It is difficult to do all these things well, simultaneously, and some actors choose to concentrate on one or two areas until they are established, and then branch out to other areas.) See *Stay Home and Star!* by William Paul Steele (Heinemann, 1992).

Since you will always be confronted with realities such as a writers' strike or fewer training video roles due to a downturn in the economy, or being the wrong type or age in any given year, generally, the more kinds of work you can do as an actor, the better your chances of making a living.

Markets Where the Work Is

Figure 15–2, "Where the Work Is," shows the top ten SAG markets, by earnings, in 1990 under all contracts. Although the table indicates that the major markets are Hollywood, New York, and Chicago, I personally know actors who make their livings exclusively in some of the medium to smaller markets like San Francisco, Boston, Seattle, and Florida. In the larger markets you are vying with more people but for presumably more numerous and better-paying jobs. In the smaller markets you are competing with fewer people for what are usually fewer and smaller jobs. However, it should be said that in the reduced economy of the 1990s, most actors I've talked to in any of the markets, big, medium, or small, are making less than they did in the 1980s and generally competing with more actors for what seem to be fewer jobs. And the benefit of earning above scale on some jobs is becoming a thing of the past.

The accompanying article, "Where The Work Is," on Figure 15–2 is from *Screen Actor* magazine, fall 1991, and is printed by permission of SAG.

Age, Gender, and Ethnicity

Age, gender, and ethnicity are all real factors in an on-camera acting career. Figure 15–3, "The Female in Focus: In Whose Image? All Feature and TV Roles Cast by Age and Sex,1989," shows the distribution of roles by contract, gender, and age. The statistical data shown in Figure 15–4, "The Female in Focus: In Whose Image? Average Annual SAG Earnings by Age and Sex, 1989," are from the fall 1990 issue of *Screen Actor* magazine. Women earned less money ($8,895 or 38 percent less) than men ($14,324) and had fewer jobs than men.

On Figure 15–5, Chart B "Screen Actors Guild 1992 Earnings by Gender," shows that in 1992 women increased their average earnings under all contracts ($10,871) by about $2,000 over 1989 but were still lagging behind the men's average of $14,138 by 24 percent. According to Rodney Mitchell, SAG Affirmative Action officer in Hollywood, women consistently make less money and have fewer jobs in any given year. He says that women earn less because they not only win fewer jobs but are paid less for those jobs than their male counterparts.

Looking again at Figure 15–3, you will see that in 1989 women earned less money than men at all ages under all contracts except for girls zero through nine years of age, who earned a tiny fraction more than boys. On the same table, you will also notice the dramatic discrepancy between men's and women's earnings from age thirty on.

Figure 15–4 shows that, during 1989, women had more work as on-camera principals in television commercials (41.4 percent) than in either theatrical feature films (29.1 percent) or television (35.4 percent). During 1991 (Figure 15–6: "Screen Actors Guild 1991 TV Commercials"; Chart A: "On-Camera Principals by Gender"), women maintained the percentage of on-camera principal roles in commercials with 41 percent of the jobs.

In Figures 15–7: "Screen Actors Guild 1992 Theatrical Films," and 15–8: "Screen Actors Guild 1992 Television," both B charts show that all women, under and over forty, made minor gains over the 1989 figures (Figure 15–3) making up 31 percent of the total performers in theatrical films and 36 percent of the total performers in television.

Like women, minority performers are also consistently underrepresented. Figure 15–9, "1989 Female Commercial Roles Cast by Ethnicity," shows that on-camera principal and off-camera (voice-over) principal roles awarded to non-Caucasian women were very meager.

Figure 15–10, "Screen Actors Guild 1991 TV Commercials," shows the number of on- and off-camera principal roles for both sexes in TV commercials by ethnicity.

The A charts in Figures 15–5, 15–7, and 15–8 also show 1992 SAG membership by ethnicity as well as the percentage of jobs in theatrical films and television by ethnicity. How do these figures reflect the diversity of real life? The 1990 U.S. Census estimates these ethnic proportions in our population:

- Caucasian   76 percent
- African American   12 percent
- Latino/Hispanic   9 percent
- Asian/Pacific   3 percent
- American Indian   1 percent

African Americans are about even in two categories of jobs during 1992 as compared to proportions in the *1990* U.S. Census: in theatrical films with 14 percent of the roles, and in television with 13 percent of the roles. In 1991, Latino/Hispanic actors had 9 percent of the off-camera principal roles in TV commercials, representing the same percentage of that population group in the *1990* U.S. Census. All other ethnic groups are underrepresented in all contracts.

The data on women and ethnic groups are discouraging. However, you should know that both SAG and AFTRA work steadily to increase employment opportunities for these groups as well as for performers with disabilities. If you're interested in helping, get involved with your local union office.

These data are not intended to discourage you but to give you the facts about the realities of making a living by acting on-camera. Smart businesspeople look at these statistical data in their markets, as should actors. It helps you realize that no matter how talented, driven, and committed you may be in your career, the numbers, the statistical data, the facts, may get in your way.

When asked what was the best advice he'd gotten as an actor, Michael York said filmmaker Franco Zeffirelli said to him, "You've got to believe in your own destiny. You've got to believe that you will succeed." When asked his response to that, York said, "That was important to hear because in the acting profession the laws of the jungle apply. And when the work comes, it's so random, there's no natural career progression, no guarantee of tenure, no gold watch at the end. An acting career is a strange mixture of anxiety and pleasure. On the one hand, the possibilities are endless, but on the other, they are just possibilities. So you have to want it a lot."

Conclusion

Acting in television commercials can be extremely creative, satisfying, and provide you with a decent day's pay or even an entire career.

When you're properly equipped with good skills, the necessary tools, and great desire, vitality, and persistence, go for it. Keep your work honest, simple, and spontaneous and have fun. (Keep your day job, too, for a while anyway.)

Whether you're new to commercials or already in the business, I hope this book has helped you improve and refine your acting skills and business knowledge. Like acting and teaching, writing this book has been a wonderful education for me. Good luck!

Where the Work Is

BY ROBERT CAIN
SAG HOLLYWOOD DIRECTOR OF RESEARCH

You have probably heard that production has resumed in New York after a long labor dispute; that Florida's film and television industries are booming; and that the real money for performers is in commercials. But did you know that the fastest growing SAG branch in the country is Washington, D.C.? Or that the average SAG commercial performer earned less in 1990, after inflation, than he or she did in 1986?

Few decisions have more impact on actors' careers than the types of work they choose to pursue, and where they pursue that work. But the entertainment industry changes so unpredictably that career planning often becomes little more than an educated guessing-game. In the interest of shedding some light on this subject, SAG's Research Department recently conducted a study of members' earnings, to determine where the work is.

The Big Picture

Even when you factor in the writers' strike of 1988, acting was a growth industry through the latter half of the 1980's. Total SAG earnings — including all session fees and residuals — grew at an annual rate of 8.1 percent, roughly mirroring the 8.4 percent annual growth in the overall filmed entertainment industry.

The composition of performers' earnings has changed considerably since 1986. Commercials were once the most important source of earnings for actors, but they now rank a distant second to television (which includes series, TV movies, mini-series and made-for-syndication shows). Theatrical film earnings are catching up, rising from just 18% of SAG earnings in 1986 to over 25% in 1990.

The reason for these shifts is a matter of simple economics. Rapid growth in the ancillary markets (e.g., videocassette, cable, foreign distribution) for American films and television programs has resulted in increased earning opportunities — and residuals — for performers. Commercial advertising, on the other hand, has been comparatively anemic, so SAG's commercial earnings — when adjusted for inflation — actually declined during the latter half of the 1980s.

Geographic Considerations

Conventional wisdom holds that New York and Los Angeles are the "best" places for performers to build and maintain their careers. Indeed, these two production centers accounted for more than 90% of SAG's record one billion dollars in total earnings in 1990. But New York and LA are clearly not the only places where work is available. Chicago, San Francisco, Florida, Washington D.C., and Detroit offer many performers the opportunity to live and work away from the harried, competitive environments of the major markets. Even the smaller cities have become sophisticated in luring location shoots to their areas. Part of Washington D.C.'s recent success, for example, is attributable to more government-themed stories and nearby Richmond, Virginia's growing popularity as an authentic backdrop for period dramas. In all, more than 17,000 members are based outside New York and Los Angeles. The adjoining chart ranks the ten largest SAG markets by members' total 1990 earnings.

Putting Things in Perspective

While the one billion dollars earned by members in 1990 may sound like a lot of money, it should be pointed out that, when apportioned out among some 78,000 active members, the figure averages to less than $13,000 per member. Of course, the true distribution of wealth is far less equitable. Only about 10% of SAG's members earned more than $25,000 from SAG work last year, and even fewer are able to consistently earn at this level year in and year out. The vast majority earn less than $3,000 in SAG in any given year, although many do earn additional income under AFTRA and Equity contracts. If there is such a thing as a "typical" SAG member, it is someone who makes a living from another occupation, and who is occasionally lucky enough to pick up a few hundred dollars from the odd commercial or character role. The myth of the "rich actor" is for most members just that, a myth. ■

★ TOP TEN SAG MARKETS ★

Branches Ranked by Total 1990 Earnings (in millions)

Branch	Earnings
Hollywood	$580m
New York	$332m
Chicago	$38m
San Francisco	$17m
Florida	$16m
Washington, D.C.	$4.9m
Detroit	$4.3m
Boston	$3.9m
Philadelphia	$3.4m
Dallas	$3.4m

Note: Earnings in all other markets totalled $17.9 mil.

Source: SAG Pension & Health data

SCREEN ACTOR / FALL 1991

Reprinted by permission of the Screen Actors Guild.

Figure 15–2 "Where the Work Is"

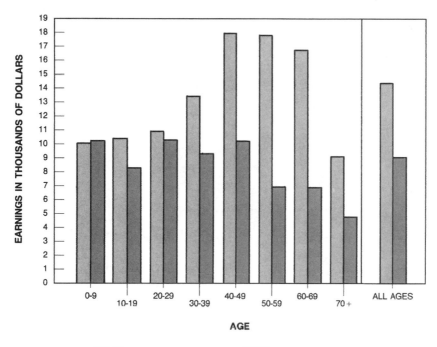

Figures represent the average session and residual earnings of SAG's 76,502 active members under all SAG contracts in calendar year 1989. Average annual SAG earnings for all members of all ages and both sexes were $12,013. Women's average earnings of $8,895 were 26% below the general average, while men's average earnings of $14,324 were 19% above the general average. In 1989, a total of 22,702 members or 30% had no earnings at all. Among SAG women, 34% or one-third had no earnings at all, while only 26% or one-quarter of SAG men had no earnings.

NOTE: That portion of each individual feature or TV salary which exceeds the Pension & Health contribution ceiling established by collective bargaining is not included in the survey. The ceilings are $200,000 for features and miniseries, $15,000 for a half-hour TV episode and $24,500 for a one-hour TV episode. There is no ceiling for commercials.

SCREEN ACTOR / FALL 1990

Figure 15–3 "The Female in Focus: In Whose Image?"

THE FEMALE IN FOCUS:

When a production company or advertiser signs a collective bargaining agreement with the Screen Actors Guild, the company agrees to "realistically portray the American scene" and to provide equal access to auditions and casting. As part of that agreement, the company provides SAG with voluntary data on the sex, age and ethnicity of performers hired.

An examination of that statistical data collected in 1989 by the SAG Affirmative Action offices in Hollywood and New York, and the earnings reported to the SAG-Producers' Pension and Health Plans in Burbank, clearly shows that female performers continue to work less and earn less than men in feature films, television and TV commercials. Those figures are charted in this report.

STAFF RESEARCH: Roger Lateiner & Tony Phipps

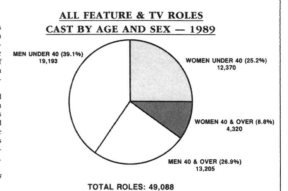

ALL FEATURE & TV ROLES
CAST BY AGE AND SEX — 1989

MEN UNDER 40 (39.1%) 19,193

WOMEN UNDER 40 (25.2%) 12,370

WOMEN 40 & OVER (8.8%) 4,320

MEN 40 & OVER (26.9%) 13,205

TOTAL ROLES: 49,088

ALL 1989 SAG ROLES CAST BY SEX

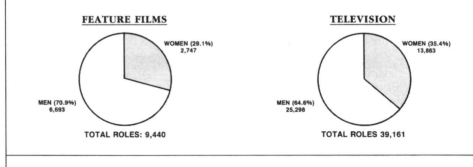

FEATURE FILMS

WOMEN (29.1%) 2,747

MEN (70.9%) 6,693

TOTAL ROLES: 9,440

TELEVISION

WOMEN (35.4%) 13,863

MEN (64.6%) 25,298

TOTAL ROLES 39,161

TV COMMERCIALS

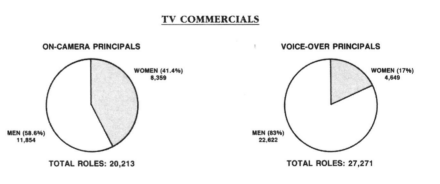

ON-CAMERA PRINCIPALS

WOMEN (41.4%) 8,359

MEN (58.6%) 11,854

TOTAL ROLES: 20,213

VOICE-OVER PRINCIPALS

WOMEN (17%) 4,649

MEN (83%) 22,622

TOTAL ROLES: 27,271

Figure 15–4 "The Female in Focus: In Whose Image"

SCREEN ACTORS GUILD

A. 1992 MEMBERSHIP BY ETHNICITY

Total   87,106

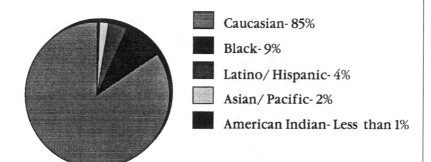

- Caucasian- 85%
- Black- 9%
- Latino/ Hispanic- 4%
- Asian/ Pacific- 2%
- American Indian- Less than 1%

B. 1992 EARNINGS BY GENDER

Total Earnings: $1,013,536,698

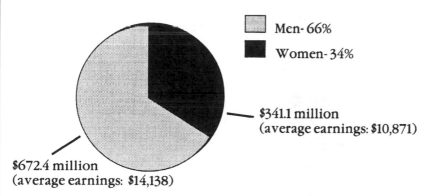

- Men- 66%
- Women- 34%

$341.1 million
(average earnings: $10,871)

$672.4 million
(average earnings: $14,138)

SAG MEMBERSHIP: 57% MALE, 43% FEMALE

Reprinted by permission of the Screen Actors Guild.

Figure 15–5 Screen Actors Guild Pie Charts

SCREEN ACTORS GUILD

1991 TV Commercials

A. ON-CAMERA PRINCIPALS BY GENDER
Total Jobs: 57,106

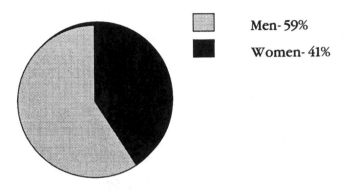

Men- 59%

Women- 41%

B. OFF- CAMERA PRINCIPALS BY GENDER
Total Jobs: 55,585

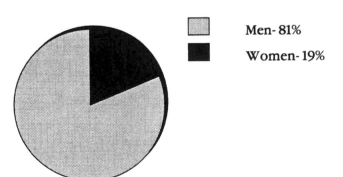

Men- 81%

Women- 19%

Figure 15–6 1991 TV Commercial Pie Charts

SCREEN ACTORS GUILD

1992 Theatrical Films

A.
BY ETHNICITY
Total Performers: 9,283

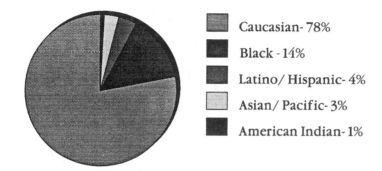

- Caucasian- 78%
- Black - 14%
- Latino/ Hispanic- 4%
- Asian/ Pacific- 3%
- American Indian- 1%

B.
BY AGE AND GENDER
Total Performers: 9,064

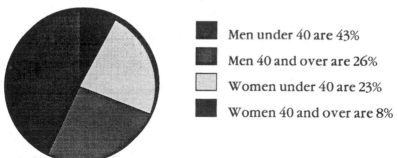

- Men under 40 are 43%
- Men 40 and over are 26%
- Women under 40 are 23%
- Women 40 and over are 8%

Reprinted by permission of the Screen Actors Guild.

Figure 15–7 1992 Theatrical Films Pie Charts

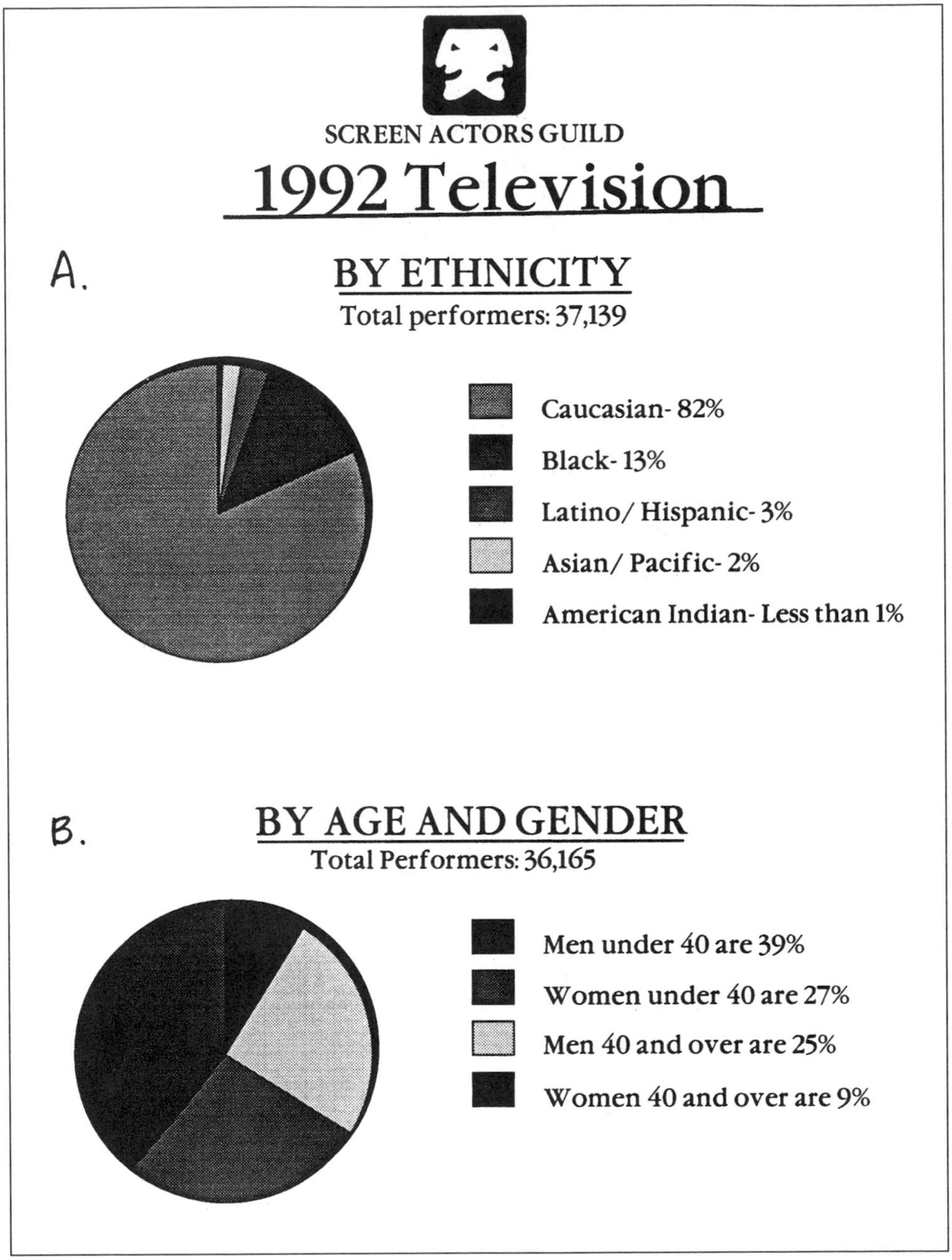

SCREEN ACTORS GUILD

1992 Television

A.

BY ETHNICITY
Total performers: 37,139

- Caucasian- 82%
- Black- 13%
- Latino/ Hispanic- 3%
- Asian/ Pacific- 2%
- American Indian- Less than 1%

B.

BY AGE AND GENDER
Total Performers: 36,165

- Men under 40 are 39%
- Women under 40 are 27%
- Men 40 and over are 25%
- Women 40 and over are 9%

Figure 15–8 1992 Television Pie Charts

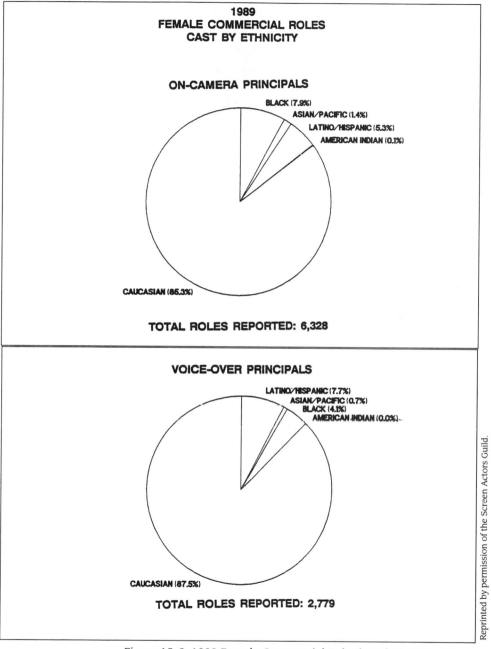

1989
FEMALE COMMERCIAL ROLES
CAST BY ETHNICITY

ON-CAMERA PRINCIPALS

BLACK (7.9%)
ASIAN/PACIFIC (1.4%)
LATINO/HISPANIC (5.3%)
AMERICAN INDIAN (0.1%)

CAUCASIAN (85.3%)

TOTAL ROLES REPORTED: 6,328

VOICE-OVER PRINCIPALS

LATINO/HISPANIC (7.7%)
ASIAN/PACIFIC (0.7%)
BLACK (4.1%)
AMERICAN INDIAN (0.0%)

CAUCASIAN (87.5%)

TOTAL ROLES REPORTED: 2,779

Figure 15–9 1989 Female Commercial Roles by Ethnicity Pie Charts

SCREEN ACTORS GUILD

1991 TV Commercials

A. ON- CAMERA PRINCIPALS BY ETHNICITY

Total Jobs: 45,802

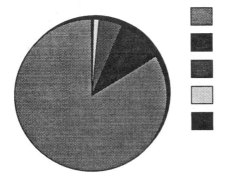

Caucasian- 84%

Black- 10%

Latino/ Hispanic- 5%

Asian/ Pacific- 1%

American Indian- Less than 1%

OFF- CAMERA PRINCIPALS BY ETHNICITY

B.

Total Jobs: 32,404

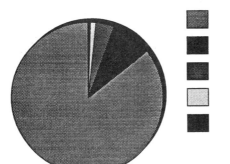

Caucasian- 86%

Latino/ Hispanic- 9%

Black- 4%

Asian/ Pacific- Less than 1%

American Indian- Less than 1%

Figure 15–10 1991 TV Commercials Pie Charts

Appendix A

COMMERCIAL COPY WITH STORYBOARDS

SAATCHI & SAATCHI   *Television Copy*

Client:	GMI	*Type:*	:30
Product:	CHEERIOS	*Show & Date:*	
Traffic No:		*Subject:*	"FARM"
Date Typed:	5/18/83		

Video   *Audio*

LITTLE GIRL: You'll never guess what <u>we</u> did!

CHORUS (VO):   Moms love Cheerios low, low sugar

                         But kids made Cheerios number one.

KIDS TOGETHER: We <u>all</u> did it.

CHORUS (VO):   Toasty oat goodness is what its got

                         One gram of sugar not alot.

<u>MOM</u>:   I love the low sugar.

                         But it's Cheerios toasted oat <u>taste</u>

                         that made it number one with my kids.

                         And part of our good breakfast.

<u>CHORUS</u> (VO): Moms love Cheerios low, low sugar

                         But <u>kids</u> made Cheerios number one.

KIDS TOGETHER: We did it!

Client's O.K.: _____   *Date:* _____   Form 30TV Rev. 6/79

Cheerios/Farm

Cheerios/Farm

Video: OPEN ON A WORKING FARM. IT'S EARLY MORNING AS TRACTOR PULLING HAY CART STOPS IN FRONT OF HOUSE.

Audio: LITTLE GIRL: You'll never guess

①

Video: LITTLE GIRL WITH WILD FLOWERS SPEAKS TO CAMERA AS SHE AND HER BROTHERS JUMP OFF CART. DAD LOOKS ON.

Audio: what we did!

②

Video: DISSOLVE AS CHEERIOS FALL INTO BOWL WITH LOGO ON IT.

Audio: But Kids made Cheerios number one

Video: CUT TO INSIDE OF HOUSE AS MOM POURS BOWLS OF CHEERIO. FAMILY COMES IN DOOR.

Audio: CHORUS (VO): Moms love Cheerios low, low sugar

③

Video: CUT TO KIDS TOSSING HATS TOWARD HAT STAND.   DAD PLACES HIS ON.

Audio: KIDS TOGETHER: We all did it.

Video:

Audio:

Date: 1/20/83
Film #
Traffic #
Page # 1 of 3
Wd.Ch.
:05

Cheerios/Farm

Cheerios/Farm

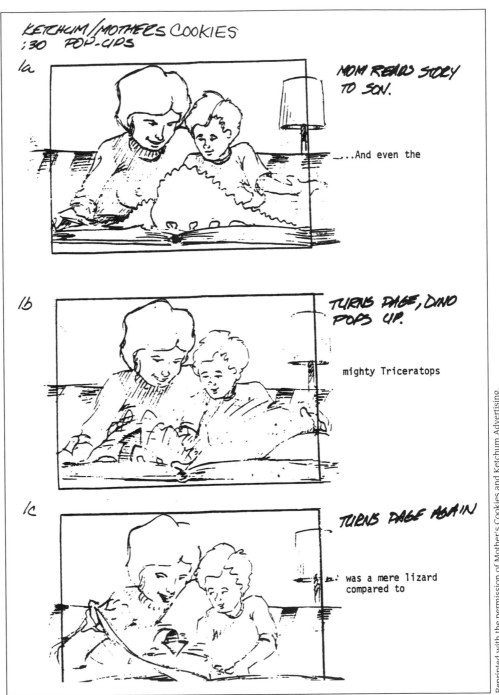

KETCHUM/MOTHER'S COOKIES
;30 POP-UPS

1a — MOM READS STORY TO SON.

...And even the

1b — TURNS PAGE, DINO POPS UP.

mighty Triceratops

1c — TURNS PAGE AGAIN

was a mere lizard compared to

Ketchum/Mother's Cookies

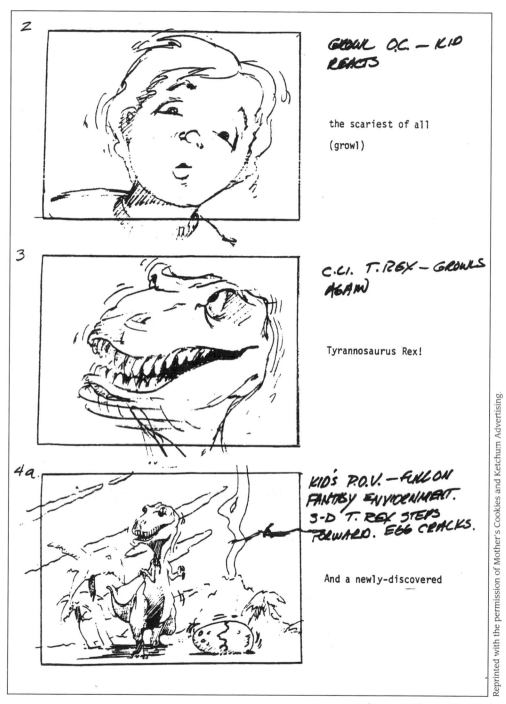

2

GROWL O.C. — KID
REACTS

the scariest of all
(growl)

3

C.U. T. REX — GROWLS
AGAIN

Tyrannosaurus Rex!

4a.

KID'S P.O.V. — FULL ON
FANTASY ENVIRONMENT.
3-D T. REX STEPS
FORWARD. EGG CRACKS.

And a newly-discovered

Ketchum/Mother's Cookies

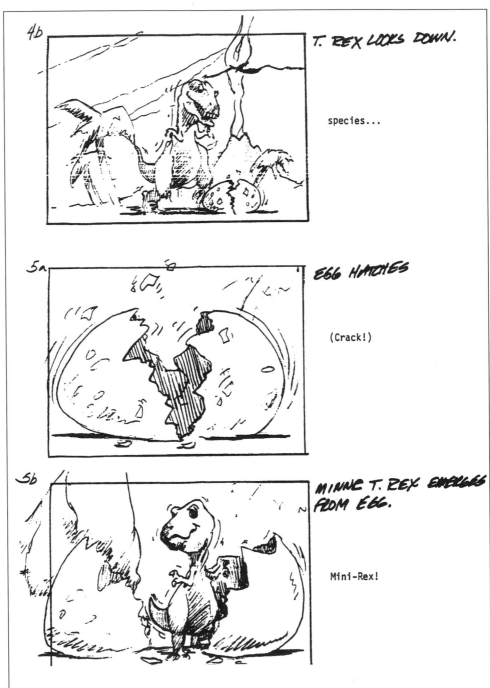

4b   T. REX LOOKS DOWN.

species...

5a   EGG HATCHES

(Crack!)

5b   MINIE T. REX EMERGES
FROM EGG.

Mini-Rex!

Ketchum/Mother's Cookies

5c — LOOKS UP & SMILES.

6a — LOW ANGLE WIDE LENS TWO SHOT. REX GROWLS

No matter
how ferocious

6b — THEN REALLY ROARS & KNOCKS TREE DOWN. IT FALLS FORWARD INTO FR.

they...

Ketchum/Mother's Cookies

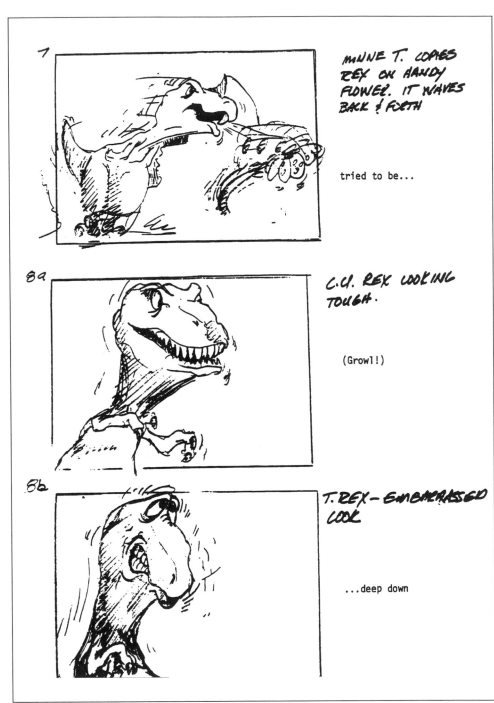

MNNE T. COPIES
REX ON HANDY
FLOWER. IT WAVES
BACK & FORTH

tried to be...

C.U. REX LOOKING
TOUGH.

(Growl!)

T. REX - EMBARRASSED
LOOK

...deep down

Ketchum/Mother's Cookies

8B — COOKIE TRANSFORMATION

they were made of

9 — KID REACHES IN FOR COOKIE

tasty graham!

10 — ANNCR VO: Bigrrr

Ketchum/Mother's Cookies

McCANN-ERICKSON, INC.
Television Commercial

Client: Coca-Cola USA/and Gillette - for Boston   Air date 3-15-82   Job #: 2-2200

Product: Sugar-Free SPRITE   Length: :30 - KODS-2302

Title: "Free Gillette Razor"   Revision #: 1

Video: Audio:

ATTRACTIVE WOMAN..
25-30 AGE RANGE
(LIMBO SETTING)

If you like getting
more for LESS..

PULL BACK. SLIGHTLY
AS SHE BRINGS UP
BOTTLE. (RAZOR NOT
YET ON IT)

sugar-free SPRITE is
the delicious way
to <u>do</u> it.

ECU, BOTTOM HALF
OF 2-LITER BOTTLE

And when you buy it
in the plastic 2-LITER
bottle .. at the regular
price ..

TILT UP AND MOVE
IN ON NECK-RINGER
RAZOR ...

you get this Gillette
Daisy SHAVER .. the
best and <u>safest</u> women's
disposable shaver ..
absolutely FREE.

Coca-Cola USA and Gillette/Sugar-Free Sprite

Title: "Free Razor" - Sugar-free Sprite   Page: -2-

Video: Audio:

SUGAR-FREE SPRITE,
POURING OVER ICE IN
GLASS WITH A "LYMON"
BY IT ...

ZOOM IN ON THE LYMON
 BY THE GLASS ...

Sugar-free Sprite is

the ONLY diet soft drink

with the cool refreshing

taste of LYMON.

WOMAN HOLDING UP BOTTLE;
NOW WITH THE FREE RAZOR
ON IT ...

And remember! When you

buy it in the plastic

2-LITER size ...

FAST ZOOM TO ECU, THE
NECK-RINGER RAZOR ON
BOTTLE ...

a free Gillette

Daisy SHAVER is

right on the

bottle.

DISPLAY OF BOTTLES WITH
NECK-RINGER RAZORS.(WITH
SUGGESTED USE OF A POS
COUNTER-CARD IN BACK-
GROUND.)AND DISCLAIMER
SUPER AT BOTTOM....

Look for special

displays and full

details where you

shop for sugar-free

SPRITE.

Coca-Cola USA and Gillette/Sugar-Free Sprite

Copy

PRINT **X**　RADIO　　　TV

CLIENT	Blue Cross Blue Shield
JOB NUMBER	BC – 413 16
JOB TITLE	1992 Advertising
SPOT TITLE	n/a
SPOT LENGTH	n/a
WRITER	REM
DATE	3/18/92
TIME	5:06 PM
PAGE	17

HMO Blue East :30 TV "Mouse" (FINAL COPY)

WAYNE:　　　I obsess about some awful thing happening to me.

I continually blow the littlest fears way out of proportion.

So I got a new health plan. HMO Blue.

This new Blue Cross and Blue Shield plan that's more affordable than their traditional plans.

There are thousands of doctors, most doctor visits are just three dollars,

and everything they cover they cover 100%.

Now nothing worries me.

Except for one thing.

Now that my fears are under control, what do I do with this cheese?

LOGO:　　　HMO Blue

A New Way Of Caring

ARNOLD FORTUNA LANE

ARNOLDFORTUNALANE INC., ADVERTISING · 420 BOYLSTON STREET, BOSTON, MA 02116 · 617-267-1900 · FAX 617-267-1987
ALBANY · BOSTON · HARTFORD · PORTLAND · ROCHESTER · SYRACUSE

Blue Cross Blue Shield/1992 Advertising

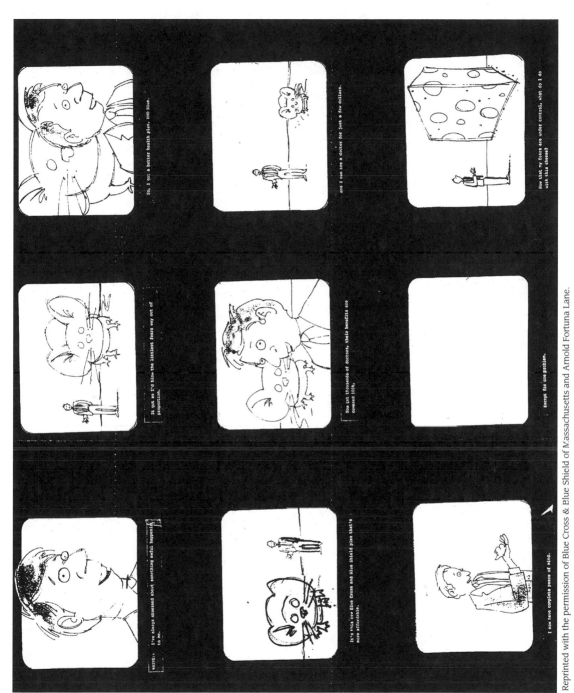

Blue Cross Blue Shield/1992 Advertising

Copy

PRINT___X___ RADIO_____ TV_____

	Blue Cross Blue Shield
CLIENT	BC – ~~413~~ 16
JOB NUMBER	1992 Advertising
JOB TITLE	n/a
SPOT TITLE	n/a
SPOT LENGTH	REM
WRITER	3/18/92
DATE	5:06 PM
TIME	20
PAGE	

HMO Blue East :30 TV "Rhino" (FINAL COPY)

WAYNE: Ever since childhood, I've been afraid of the dark.

I'd feel something awful was going to get me.

Let me show you how I got over it.

I got this new health plan. HMO Blue.

This new Blue Cross and Blue Shield plan that's more
affordable than their traditional plans.

There are thousands of doctors, most doctor visits
are just three dollars,

and everything they cover they cover 100%.

Now my fears are gone. And the dark, well that's
just my imagination.

OK, let's try this again.

LOGO: HMO Blue   A New Way Of Caring

ARNOLD FORTUNA LANE

ARNOLDFORTUNALANE INC., ADVERTISING · 420 BOYLSTON STREET, BOSTON, MA 02116 · 617-267-1900 · FAX 617-267-1987
ALBANY · BOSTON · HARTFORD · PORTLAND · ROCHESTER · SYRACUSE

Blue Cross Blue Shield/1992 Advertising

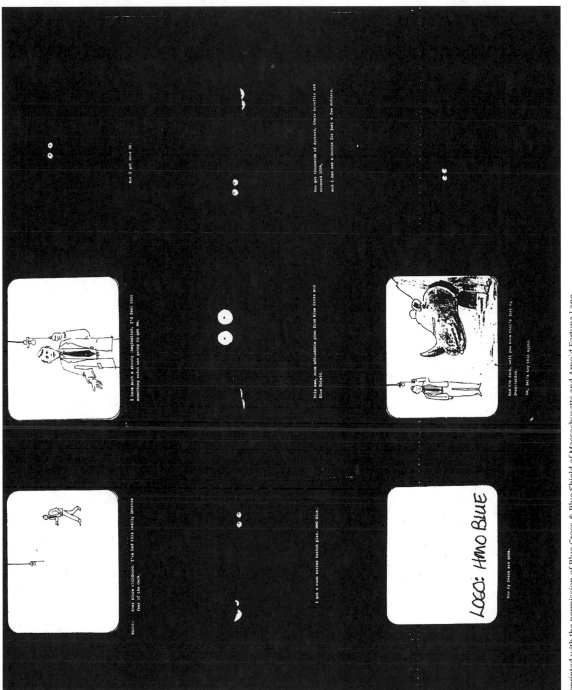

Blue Cross Blue Shield/1992 Advertising

Blue Cross Blue Shield/1992 Advertising

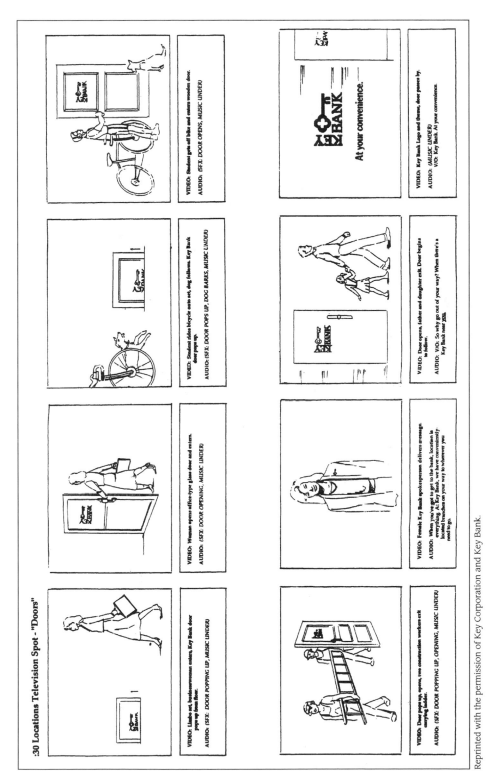

Television Spot "Doors"

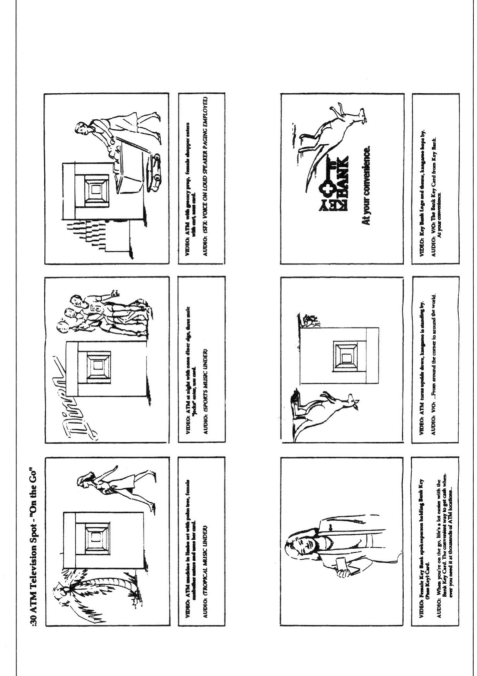

:30 ATM Television Spot - "On the Go"

ATM Television Spot "On the Go"

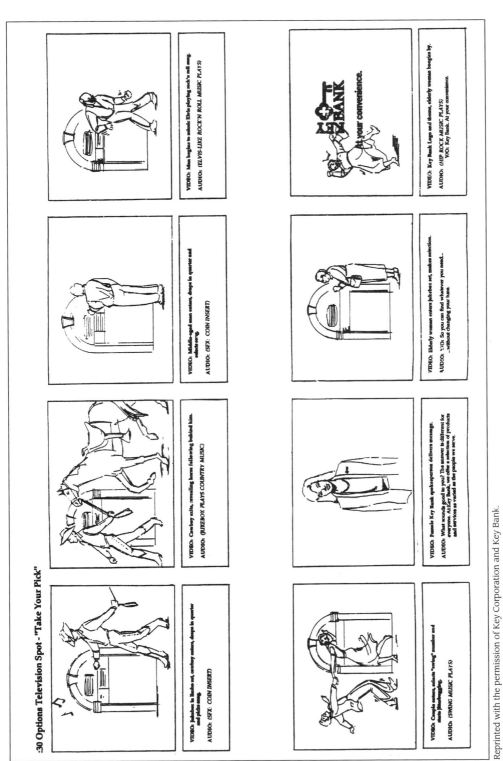

:30 Options Television Spot - "Take Your Pick"

VIDEO: Jukebox in Insides set, cowboy enters, drops in quarter and picks song.

AUDIO: (SFX: COIN INSERT)

VIDEO: Cowboy exits, revealing horse (following behind him).

AUDIO: (JUKEBOX PLAYS COUNTRY MUSIC)

VIDEO: Middle-aged man enters, drops in quarter and selects song.

AUDIO: (SFX: COIN INSERT)

VIDEO: Man begins to animate Elvis playing rock'n roll song.

AUDIO: (ELVIS-LIKE ROCK'N ROLL MUSIC PLAYS)

VIDEO: Couple enters, selects "swing" number and starts jitterbugging.

AUDIO: (SWING MUSIC PLAYS)

VIDEO: Female Key Bank spokesperson delivers message.

AUDIO: What sounds good to you? The answer is different for everyone. At Key Bank, we offer a selection of products and services as varied as the people we serve.

VIDEO: Elderly woman enters jukebox set, makes selection.

AUDIO: V/O: So you can find whatever you need... ...without changing your tune.

VIDEO: Key Bank Logo and theme, elderly woman boogies by.

AUDIO: (HIP ROCK MUSIC PLAYS)
V/O: Key Bank. At your convenience.

Television Spot "Take Your Pick"

Appendix B

COMMERCIAL COPY WITHOUT STORYBOARDS

BLUE CROSS &
BLUE SHIELD OF RI
BC-472-h
APRIL 12, 1991
"Doctor...Uh"/TV :30

(A woman getting her hair done is subjected to the hairdresser's opinion concerning what doctor she should see.)

Woman: SO ANYWAY, WHAT YOU'VE GOT IS JUST EXACTLY LIKE THIS GALL BLADDER THING WITH MY MOTHER-IN-LAW...

SHE WAS GOING TO THIS ONE GUY... "LOOK, " I SAID, "TRY THIS OTHER GUY... HE'S GREAT, HE'S THE BEST,

HE'S A VERY, VERY, DEAR FRIEND OF MINE." DOCTOR... UH, DOCTOR... UH...

VO: SOONER OR LATER, YOU'LL HEAR A LOT ABOUT WHAT DOCTOR YOU SHOULD GO TO.

FORTUNATELY, WITH HEALTHMATE FROM BLUE CROSS, YOU CAN CHOOSE ANY DOCTOR YOU WANT.

Woman: DOCTOR... UH, DOCTOR... UH...

VO: HEALTHMATE. FROM BLUE CROSS AND BLUE SHIELD.

Reprinted with permission. Agency: Pagano Schenck & Kay, Client: Blue Cross & Blue Shield of Rhode Island.

Blue Cross & Blue Shield of Rhode Island/"Doctor . . .Uh"

 **LEO BURNETT U.S.A.**

35 WEST WACKER DRIVE, CHICAGO, ILLINOIS 606•
(312) 220-5959

KELLOGG COMPANY
30-Second Film
"TEEN CRUNCH/REVISED"
CORN FLAKES
KLCF9973

Approved For Bidding: 10/15/91 mb
Revision #1:   10/15/91 mb

Job #: P18992

<u>VIDEO</u>

<u>AUDIO</u>

1 OPEN ON TITLE: "INTRODUCING A
CEREAL FROM KELLOGG'S". DIS-
SOLVE TO TEEN IN HIS ENVIRON-
MENT. SUPER: "INTRODUCING A
CEREAL FROM KELLOGG'S".

KID: Flakes? What can I say? I mea
they look kinda stupid just
sittin' there. Duh!

2 TEEN POKES AT BOWL WITH SPOON.

Lights out - nobody's home. No
fruit, no raisins, no nothing!

3 TEEN TASTES CEREAL.

Hey wait.

4 CUT TO PRODUCT FALLING IN SUPER
SLOW MOTION.

There's something about these.
It's the taste.

5 CUT BACK TO TEEN.

Yeah. It's kinda crunchy. Kinda
good. Hey! I like 'em.

6 CUT BACK TO PRODUCT. WE SEE
MILK POUR AND SUPER: "KELLOGG'S
CORN FLAKES".

AVO: Kellogg's Corn Flakes.

7 CUT BACK TO TEEN AS HE'S SUR-
PRISED TO DISCOVER IT'S
KELLOGG'S CORN FLAKES.

KID: Kellogg's Corn Flakes! Duh!

8 CUT TO PACKAGE OF KELLOGG'S CORN
FLAKES WITH BOWL OF CEREAL AND
END SUPER: "TASTE THEM AGAIN FOR
THE FIRST TIME". SUPER: "®1991
KELLOGG COMPANY". SUPER:
"®KELLOGG COMPANY".

AVO: Taste them again for the first
time.

Kellogg Company/"TEEN CRUNCH/REVISED"

JUN 09 '92 09:16 LEO BURNETT

LEO BURNETT U.S.A.

35 WEST WACKER DRIVE, CHICAGO, ILLINOIS 60601
(312) 720-6859

P.3

KELLOGG COMPANY
30-Second Film
"MUSCLES"
CORN FLAKES
KLCF9963

Approved For Bidding: 10/15/91   vls

Job #: P18992

	VIDEO	AUDIO
1	OPEN ON TITLE: "INTRODUCING A CEREAL FROM KELLOGG'S." DISSOLVE TO MAN IN HIS ENVIRONMENT.	MAN: Flakes...just flakes? A little wimpy. Don't ya think? C'mon...Who'd wanna eat this?
2	MAN TASTES CEREAL.	Hold it...Hold on now...These do pack a good crunch.
3	CUT TO PRODUCT FALLING IN SUPER SLOW MOTION.	They taste good...Real down to earth.
4	CUT TO MAN AS HE CONTINUES TO TALK AND EAT CEREAL.	Substantial. Yup. I like these alright. They've got some muscle.
5	CUT BACK TO PRODUCT. WE SEE MILK POUR AND SUPER: "KELLOGG'S CORN FLAKES."	AVO: Kellogg's Corn Flakes.
6	CUT BACK TO MAN AS HE'S SURPRISED TO DISCOVER IT'S KELLOGG'S CORN FLAKES.	MAN: Kellogg's Corn Flakes? (SURPRISED VOICE) Ehem...(DEEP VOICE) Kellogg's Corn Flakes.
7	CUT TO PACKAGE OF KELLOGG'S CORN FLAKES WITH BOWL OF CEREAL AND END SUPER: "TASTE THEM AGAIN FOR THE FIRST TIME." SUPER: "©1991 KELLOGG COMPANY." SUPER: "©KELLOGG COMPANY."	AVO: Taste them again for the first time.

Kellogg Company/"MUSCLES"

Outcasting, inc.

CENTRAL MAINE POWER

AUDITION MAY 4,1991

Anncr: You claim you can see into.........

Guesser: ..dont tell me...the future!

Anncr: (holds up electric bill) Okay, Predict your monthly electric
          bill from CMP ?

Guesser: (Whispers into ear of Anncr:)

Anncr: (Opens envelope--Incredulous).....Thats amazing!

Guesser: (Smugly nods to indicate" no"); CMP's Budget Payment Plan.

Anncr: Budget Payment Plan?

Guesser: Averages my monthly electric usage....so I always pay the same.
Cold snaps in the winter,unexpected guests, my bill's always the same.

Anncr: Sounds like CMP's budget plan takes the....guesswork out of
paying your.........

Guesser: Dont tell me....electric bills.

Central Maine Power

Creative Design & Marketing, Inc.
1/3/91

Central Maine Power
LOW INCOME TV :30

Revised 1/4/91

CMP has good news for low-income families struggling with electric bills. If you use electricity to heat your home or hot water, CMP has special insulation programs that will really lower your bills. They're free to low-income families, CMP does all the work, and you'll save money right away. Even your apartment may qualify. Call the number shown and ask for CMP's free insulation programs.

(super 1-800-8-SAY-YES)

Budget by Monday 1/14

Central Maine Power/Low Income TV

DRAKES

TIMES ARE TOUGH TODAY, RIGHT? PRICES KEEP GOING UP....AND UP....

AND UP. WANT TO HEAR SOME GOOD NEWS FOR A CHANGE? AT

DRAKE'S, WE'RE BRINGING OUR PRICES DOWN. SO NOW YOU GET

THOSE SAME DELICIOUS DEVIL DOGS, RING DINGS, YANKEE DOODLES

AND MORE. . . FOR LESS. AT DRAKE'S, ALL WE CHANGED WAS THE

PRICE. AND FOR MY MONEY, THAT'S A CHANGE FOR THE BETTER.

Drakes

Appendix | C

BEFORE AND AFTER: STORYBOARDS AND PICTUREBOARDS

CABOT ADVERTISING

Client ___NEW ENGLAND TELEPHONE___ Job No. __TEL-3414__ Date __4/28/88__
Title ___"The Family"___ Length __:30__ Page __1__ of __4__

.udio:

RONNIE:

Hi, Mom, Hi, Dad.

DAD:

How's the new apartment?

RONNIE:

I love it. (CLEARS HER THROAT) Look... uh... I'm thinking of talking to Jill.

MOM:

Jill?

CLICK OF PHONE BEING PUT DOWN.

New England Telephone/"The Family" Storyboard

CABOT ADVERTISING

Client __NEW ENGLAND TELEPHONE__   Job No. __TEL-3414__   Date __4/28/88__

Title ____"The Family"____   Length ___:30___   Page _2_ of _4_

lio:

RONNIE: (QUICKLY)

Hello . . . Mom?

MOM:

I'm here. You know he doesn't like to talk about your sister.

RONNIE:

That's the trouble. . .

RONNIE:

. . . he won't talk about her.

New England Telephone/"The Family" Storyboard

New England Telephone/"The Family" Storyboard

CABOT ADVERTISING

Client ____NEW ENGLAND TELEPHONE____ Job No. _TEL-3414_____ Date _4/28/88_____

Title ____"The Family"_____ Length ___:30_____ Page_4_____ of __4___

.udio:

RONNIE:

We're going to have
to start talking,
Mom.

SINGERS:

We're the one for
you New England.
New England Telephone.

ANNCR: (VO)

Part of the
NYNEX Family.

New England Telephone/"The Family" Storyboard

New England Telephone/"The Apology" Storyboard

CABOT ADVERTISING

Client ___NEW ENGLAND TELEPHONE___ Job No. ___TEL-3414___ Date __4/19/88__

Title ___"The Apology"___ Length __:30__ Page __2__ of __4__

DAD:

I still can't believe she left like that.

VERONICA:

Well, you didn't give her much choice.

DAD: (EMOTIONAL)

She had a choice. Him or her family.

VERONICA: (SOFTLY)

That's not a choice. It's an ultimatum.

New England Telephone/"The Apology" Storyboard

CABOT ADVERTISING

Client ___NEW ENGLAND TELEPHONE___ Job No. ___TEL-3414___ Date ___4/19/88___

Title ___"The Apology"___ Length ___:30___ Page ___3___ of ___4___

DAD: (DEEP SIGH) (PAUSE)

VERONICA:

You miss her, don't you?

DAD:

I've thought about her every day for two years.

VERONICA:

(SHE SENSES HIS EMOTION, AND SOFTLY SAYS...)
Oh, Dad.

New England Telephone/"The Apology" Storyboard

CABOT ADVERTISING

Client ___ NEW ENGLAND TELEPHONE ___ Job No. ___ TEL-3414 ___ Date __ 4/19/88 __

Title _____ "The Apology" _____ Length ___ :30 ___ Page _ 4 _ of _ 4 _

SINGERS:

We're the one for
you New England.
New England Telephone.

ANNCR:

Part of the
NYNEX Family.

New England Telephone/"The Apology" Storyboard

1988 NEW ENGLAND TELEPHONE ADVERTISING RESIDENCE USAGE CAMPAIGN PART I
PART ONE

:30

KATHY: Hi, Mom. Hi, Dad.

MOM: Hi, darling.
DAD: Kathy, how's the apartment?

KATHY: Oh, I love it! Look, I talked to Jill.

(SOUND OF PHONE RECEIVER HANGING UP)
KATHY: Hello?

MOM: I'm here. You know he doesn't like to talk about your sister.

KATHY: It's been two years now.

MOM: I know, but . . .

KATHY: Mom, we all have to start talking.

SINGERS: WE'RE THE ONE FOR YOU NEW ENGLAND, NEW ENGLAND TELEPHONE.

DATE: JUNE 29, 1988

1988 New England Telephone Ad Part I/"The Family" Pictureboard

1988 NEW ENGLAND TELEPHONE ADVERTISING RESIDENCE USAGE CAMPAIGN PART II

PART II   :30

DAD: Kathy, I want to apologize for hanging up on you.

KATHY: That's o. k., Dad.

DAD: I don't like to talk about your sister.
KATHY: I know.

DAD: I still can't believe she left like that.

KATHY: Well, you didn't give her much choice. You really miss her, don't you?

Oh, Dad.

SINGERS: WE'RE THE ONE FOR YOU NEW ENGLAND, NEW ENGLAND TELEPHONE.

DATE: JUNE 29, 1988

1988 New England Telephone Ad Part II/"The Family" Pictureboard

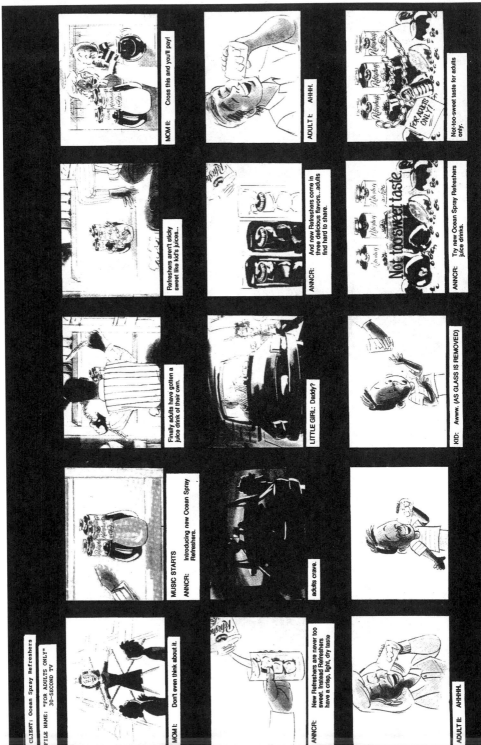

Ocean Spray Refreshers/"For Adults Only" Storyboard

Ocean spray

Refreshers
Juice Drinks ™

"FOR ADULTS ONLY" :30

KIDS: Mommy...

MOM I: Don't even think about it.

(MUSIC UP)
ANNCR: Introducing new Ocean Spray Refreshers.

Finally adults have gotten a juice drink of their own.

Refreshers aren't sticky sweet like kid's juice drinks...

MOM II: Cross this and you'll pay!

ANNCR: New Refreshers are never too sweet. Instead Refreshers have a crisp, light, dry taste adults crave.

LITTLE GIRL: Daddy?

ANNCR: And new Refreshers come in three delicious flavors...

adults...

find hard

to share.

ANNCR: Try new

Ocean Spray Refreshers juice drinks. Not-too-sweet taste for adults only.

Ocean Spray Refreshers/"For Adults Only" Pictureboard

Appendix D

PICTUREBOARDS

Polaroid OneFilm

"SAFARI"
PD OF 0283

Length: 30 seconds

(NOT SPOKEN)
OneFilm presents
"The Simple Photographer."

I stalk the wild gorilla

careful not to be noticed.

He moves in and out of the light.

But with 35MM OneFilm from Polaroid

I can capture the majestic creature

in low light, bright light inside or out.

With the same roll of OneFilm, I can
shoot under almost any conditions.

(SFX: GORILLA NOISE)

ANNCR: 35MM OneFilm. The simple
choice. From Polaroid.

Ahh, the thrill of safari.
(HORN HONKING)

DRIVER: Next stop is the polar bear -
Wait!

Polaroid/"Safari" Pictureboard

Polaroid OneFilm

"Chart"
PDOF 9193

Length: 30 seconds

ANNCR. V.O.: Buying 35mm film can be confusing.
SALESMAN #1: It's not confusing.
CUSTOMER: It's not?

SALESMAN #2: Look at our simple chart.

CUSTOMER: Chart?
SALESMAN #2: There's 100.

SALESMAN #1: You use it here.
SALESMAN #2: But not here.
SALESMAN #1: There's 400.

SALESMAN #2: Use it here.
SALESMAN #1: Or there.
SALESMAN #2: Not here.

SALESMAN #1: And there.
SALESMAN #2: There's 1000
SALESMAN #1: Don't use it here or here.

SALESMAN #2: Just there.
SALESMEN #1 & 2: See?

CUSTOMER: I see.

ANNCR. V.O.: Introducing 35MM Polaroid OneFilm. With OneFilm, you can get beautiful pictures,

here, there, or

just about anywhere.

New 35mm OneFilm. For beautiful pictures, the choice is easy.

Polaroid/"Chart" Pictureboard

Polaroid OneFilm

"Advice"
PDOF 9203

Length: 30 seconds

ANNCR. V.O.: Choosing 35mm film is never easy.

CUSTOMER: I'm confused.

SALESMAN #1: It's all very simple.
CUSTOMER: Oh.
SALESMAN #2: There's 100.

SALESMAN #1: For inside and out.
SALESMAN #2: Unless it's too dark or too bright.

SALESMAN #1: And then change to 400.
SALESMAN #2: Or you could push it to 800.

SALESMAN #1: If you don't mind the grain.
SALESMAN #2: But it is faster.

SALESMAN #1: Depending on the conditions.
SALESMAN #2: Well then you use 1000.
SALESMAN #1: Of course.

CUSTOMER: Change to 400?

ANNCR. V.O.: Introducing 35mm Polaroid OneFilm. With OneFilm you can get beautiful pictures,

in bright light, low light,

inside and out.

New 35mm OneFilm. For beautiful pictures, the choice is easy.

Polaroid/"Advice" Pictureboard

TUMS.

:30 TV COMMERCIAL "CARNIVAL"

ANNCR: You rode the

same rides...

Ate the same junk.

Got the same heartburn!

But his antacid's different from yours!

His Tums has calcium. Most antacids don't.

Regular Rolaids uses an aluminum salt.

This uses aluminum and magnesium.

So does this.

Of all these, only Tums helps wipe out heartburn and gives you calcium you need every day!

© 1992 SmithKline Beecham Consumer Brands

MOM: Something my body needs anyway...I like that!

AVO: Calcium rich Tums.

Agency: Jordan, McGrath, Case & Taylor Inc.

Tums/"Carnival" Pictureboard

SUCRETS
"SKATING RINK" :30

CLIENT: SMITHKLINE BEECHAM

COMM'L NO.: BEST 2013

DAUGHTER: C'mon, Daddy, c'mon!
DAD: No, you go ahead, honey.

DAD: My throat really hurts...

MOM: Aw...honey, try this. It really
works.

ANNCR VO: When your throat feels raw
and scratchy, take Sucrets.

Because only Sucrets

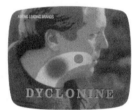

has the medicine Dyclonine,

to soothe minor sore throat pain for
long-lasting relief.

Try Sucrets. It wraps your throat

in soothing relief.
DAD: Much better!

DAUGHTER: Yea!! C'mon Daddy, c'mon!

MOM: Hey, wait for me!

ANNCR VO: Sucrets...wraps your throat
in soothing relief.

Sucrets/"Skating Rink" Pictureboard

30-Second Commercial: "Concert Tickets/Guarantee"

GIRL #1: Great seats, Row C!

GIRL #2: That's...down front? ...Right?

GIRL #1: Please!

GIRL #2: Great! Maybe they'll put a huge spotlight on my zits!

GIRL #1: There won't be any zits. You're gonna OXYcute 'em!

ANNCR: Pimples?

OXYcute 'em

with Oxy 10.

So strong, even a

dermatologist couldn't prescribe

a stronger level of benzoyl peroxide.

Oxy helps clear pimples away

or you don't pay.

(SEAL ZOOMS IN) Guaranteed.

GIRL #2: OXYcute 'em

(SUPER FLASHES ON SCREEN: OXYCUTE 'EM)

© 1991 SmithKline Beecham Consumer Brands

Agency: Jordan, McGrath, Case & Taylor, Inc.

Oxy10/"Concert Tickets/Guarantee" Pictureboard

BBDO

Batten, Barton, Durstine & Osborn, Inc.

Client: GE CORPORATE   Time: 30 SECONDS

Product: MEDICAL SYSTEMS   Title: "EXCUSES"   Comml. No.: GEDO-9083

WOMAN 1: "I have to cancel."
WOMAN 2: "I keep cancelling."

WOMAN 3: "I had to cancel."

WOMAN 4: "Why do you keep putting it off?"
WOMAN 5: "Mother, I'm not . . ."

AVO: GE's breast cancer detection system.

WOMAN 6: "I keep meaning to."

WOMAN 7: "Did you go?"
WOMAN 8: "I'm too busy. I'm too busy."

AVO: It can help detect tumors too tiny to be felt.

WOMAN 9: "I have such a busy week. I'm going to go next week."

WOMAN 10: "I can't find the time."
WOMAN 11: "I just haven't had time."

WOMAN 12: "When?"

AVO: It can increase the survival rate to 91%.

WOMAN 13: "I'll go when I have the time."

WOMAN 14: "Next week."
WOMAN 15: "Oh, I can't next week."

WOMAN 13: "Don't start with me."
WOMAN 16: "As soon as I can find the time, I'll go."

AVO: But there's one thing GE can't do. We can't make you go.

SUPER: A mammogram. Don't put it off.
WOMAN 17: "It's nothing to worry about. I just couldn't go."

General Electric/"Excuses" Pictureboard

BBDO
Batten, Barton, Durstine & Osborn, Inc.

Client: GE CORPORATE | | | Time: 60 Seconds
Product: TUNGSRAM | Title: "HUNGARIAN RHAPSODY" | | Comml. No: GEDO 0086

(MUSIC: LISZT'S
"HUNGARIAN RHAPSODY")

MAN #1: Freedom's all that
matters. Freedom
is everything.

ANNCR. V.O.: There's a
new light shining over
Eastern Europe.

MAN #2: The Hungarians are
waiting for a very long time.

ANNCR. V.O.: A light of
hope, joy, and most of all,
a new light of freedom.

WOMAN #1: Everything is
changing. It's wonderful.

MAN #3: It's a miracle.
WOMAN #2: I'm so happy.

ANNCR. V.O.: And in this
spirit, GE has entered into
an historic partnership

with a company called
Tungsram, Hungary's leading
lighting company.

(MUSIC)

MAN #4: Freedom is
something that you have to
work for very hard.

WOMAN #3: It's like a dream.
A beautiful dream.
(MUSIC)

ANNCR. V.O.: At GE
we're proud to play even a
small part in helping

the Hungarian people build
what promises to be
a truly brilliant future.

WOMAN #4: I feel
young again.

(MUSIC)

General Electric/"Hungarian Rhapsody" Pictureboard

BBDO

Batten, Barton, Durstine & Osborn, Inc.

Client: GE CORPORATE

Product: MEDICAL SYSTEMS

Title: "PREPARE A CHILD"

Time: 60 SECONDS

Comml. No.: GEDO 9056

(MUSIC)
CHILD: Is it going to be scary?

AVO: There was a time when you
had to prepare a child for
exploratory surgery.

CHILD: Will you stay there with me?

AVO: Calm his fears. Soothe his
anxieties.
CHILD: Mom, I want to go home.

DOCTOR: Come in.

AVO: Comfort him when he
imagined the worst.

CHILD: Can I bring Sam?

DOCTOR: Sure.

AVO: Well, today it's a lot easier
because the exploratory can be
performed without a scalpel,

without anesthesia, even without a
hospital stay. If it's performed by the
Magnetic Resonance Imager,

developed by GE. A remarkably
simple way to give doctors a clear
picture of problems

that could only be diagnosed before
with conventional surgery.

DOCTOR: It's not serious, he'll be
fine.

MOTHER: Ready to go home?
AVO: The MR Imager from GE. It
makes looking inside the human
body easier for everyone.

CHILD: See Sam, that wasn't so
bad.
AVO: GE. We bring good things to
life.

General Electric/"Prepare a Child" Pictureboard

Appendix E

SCREEN ACTORS GUILD AND
AFTRA OFFICES

SAG NATIONAL HEADQUARTERS
Museum Square
5757 Wilshire Boulevard
Los Angeles, CA 90036-3600
(213) 954-1600

AFTRA NATIONAL HEADQUARTERS
260 Madison Avenue
New York, NY 10016
(212) 532-0800

ARIZONA

SAG & AFTRA
1616 E. Indian School Rd.
Suite 330
Phoenix, AZ 85016
(602) 265-2712
(800) 308-2712

BOSTON

SAG & AFTRA
11 Beacon St., Suite 512
Boston, MA 02108
(617) 742-2688

CHICAGO

SAG & AFTRA
75 E. Wacker Dr.
14th Floor
Chicago, IL 60601
(312) 372-8081

CINCINNATI/COLUMBUS/DAYTON/LOUISVILLE

AFTRA
128 East 6th Ave.
Suite 802
Cincinnati, OH 45202
(513) 579-8668

CLEVELAND

SAG & AFTRA
1030 Euclid Ave., #429
Cleveland, OH 44115
(216) 781-2255

DALLAS/FORT WORTH

SAG & AFTRA
6060 North Central Expressway
Suite 302
LB 604
Dallas, TX 75206
(214) 363-8300

COLORADO, NEVADA, NEW MEXICO, and UTAH

SAG & AFTRA
950 S. Cherry St.
Suite 502
Denver, CO 80222
(303) 757-6226
(800) 527-7517

DETROIT

SAG & AFTRA
28690 S. Field Rd.
Lathrop Village, MI 48076
(810) 559-9540

FLORIDA

SAG
7300 N. Kendall
Suite 620
Miami, FL 33156
(305) 670-7677

AFTRA
20401 NW 2nd Ave.
Suite 102
Miami, FL 33169
(305) 652-4824

GEORGIA

SAG & AFTRA
455 E. Paces Ferry
Suite 334
Atlanta, GA 30305
(404) 239-0131

HAWAII

SAG & AFTRA
949 Kapiolani Blvd.
Honolulu, HI 96814
(808) 538-6122

HOUSTON

SAG & AFTRA
2650 Fountain View
Suite 326
Houston, TX 77057
(713) 972-1806

KANSAS CITY

AFTRA
4000 Baltimore, 2nd Floor
P.O. Box 32167
Kansas City, MO 64171
(816) 753-4557

LOS ANGELES

AFTRA
6922 Hollywood Blvd.
8th Floor
P.O. Box 4070
Hollywood, CA 90078-6128
(213) 461-8111

MINNEAPOLIS/ST. PAUL

SAG & AFTRA
708 North First St.
Suite 343A
Minneapolis, MI 55401
(612) 371-9120

NASHVILLE

SAG & AFTRA
1108 17th Avenue South
Nashville, TN 37212
(615) 327-2958

NEW ORLEANS

AFTRA
2475 Canal St.
Suite 108
New Orleans, LA 70119
(504) 822-6568

NEW YORK

SAG
1515 Broadway
44th Floor
New York, NY 10036
(212) 944-1030

ORLANDO

SAG
3393 W. Vine St.
Kissimmee, FL 34741
(407) 847-4445

PHILADELPHIA

SAG & AFTRA
230 S. Broad St.
10th Floor
Philadelphia, PA 19102
(215) 732-0507

PITTSBURG

AFTRA
Fleet 2007, Penthouse
625 Stanwycks St.
Pittsburg, PA 15222
(412) 281-6767

PORTLAND

AFTRA
516 SE Morrison
Suite M3
Portland, OR 97214
(503) 238-6914

SAN DIEGO

SAG & AFTRA
7827 Convoy Ct., #400
San Diego, CA 92111
(619) 278-7695

SAN FRANCISCO

SAG & AFTRA
235 Pine
San Francisco, CA 94104
(415) 391-7510

SEATTLE

SAG & AFTRA
601 Valley St., #200
Seattle, WA 98109
(206) 282-2506

ST. LOUIS

SAG & AFTRA
906 Olive
Suite 1006
St. Louis, MO 63101
(314) 231-8410

WASHINGTON, DC/BALTIMORE

SAG & AFTRA
5480 Wisconsin Ave.
Suite 201
Chevy Chase, MD 20815
(301) 657-2560

"Action": The verbal cue indicating the camera is rolling and that you, the actor, should begin your performance.

AD: Assistant Director. First AD works for and with the director. Sets shots, translates director's wishes and technical orders. Second AD is assistant to the Assistant Director. Schedules actors' call times, handles talent, handles extras.

Ad Agency: Where the concepts for and writing of commercials take place. The ad agency production team usually consists of an account executive/ manager/supervisor, a copywriter, a producer, and an art director. The actual production/filming is subcontracted to production houses.

AEA: Actors' Equity Association is the labor union encompassing all professional performers in the legitimate theatre in the United States.

AFTRA: American Federation of Television and Radio Artists. The union that represents performers, including newscasters and announcers in live and taped TV shows, radio spots, recordings, and videotaped commercials and educational industrials/corporate videos.

Agent: The actor's representative. A talent agent approved by AFTRA or SAG to solicit and negotiate employment for their members. The agent must sign a contract with the appropriate union(s), thus becoming "franchised." If an agent is not franchised, s/he is not "legit"; s/he cannot negotiate actors' contracts with union productions, nor can s/he take a commission.

Art Director: Person who conceives and designs the sets, usually on a commercial.

This glossary is reprinted courtesy of Boston AFTRA/SAG with special thanks to Executive Director Dona Sommers and SAG board member Gene Boles.

Audition: A tryout for a role in front of a casting director, director, or client for which a reading or improvisation is required. There must be a sign-in sheet for your name and a space for sign-in and sign-out times. Under most contracts, the agency or producer cannot hold you for longer than an hour at a first audition without paying you.

Availability: Inquiry by producer to see if you are free for a particular day or time period to do a job.

Blocking: The physical movements given by the director for actors to perform in any scene.

Booking: A firm commitment to hire a performer to do a specific job. "I'd like to book you for this job. The booking is for this date. Consider yourself booked."

Boom: A microphone, usually on an extended pole.

Breakdown: A detailed listing and description of roles available for casting in a production.

Buyout: Payment to an extra or hand model for a session fee with no residual payments required.

Callback: Any follow-up interview or audition after the initial audition.

Call Sheet: A production company's daily listing of schedule, scene, and cast involved.

Call Time: The time you are to arrive on the set.

Casting Director: A person or agency contracted by a client to bring in actors to audition for the client's project. The casting director is hired by and works for the client, not the actor.

Casting Call: An audition. Can be held by an advertising agency, producer, or casting director.

Cheat: A direction that means to move your head or body slightly toward or away from the camera. "Cheat a little to the left," for example. You can also cheat furniture and props.

Client: The company that contracts to have a job done.

CU or Close-Up: Camera term for tight shot (shoulders and face).

Cold Reading: Unrehearsed reading of a scene at auditions.

Commission: Percentage of performer's earnings paid to agents or managers for services rendered. Only franchised agents are allowed to take a commission.

Composite: Several contrasting photos (usually four) on an 8 × 10.

Conflict or Exclusivity: As an on-camera principal player in a specific commercial, you may not accept a job as an on-camera principal in a commercial for a competing product for as long as you are being held on the first commercial. If you have a Coke commercial running or on hold, you can't do Pepsi. A product can also be a company like Black & Decker or AT&T.

Copy: The script for a radio or TV commercial. Also used loosely to refer to any writing for TV or radio.

CSA: Casting Society of America, an organization for casting directors.

Cue: A verbal or physical signal to tell talent or crew when to proceed with action.

Cue Card: A large poster-size card with copy written on it in large letters; it is used mostly for auditions and sometimes for on-air programs.

Cut: Any deletion from the original script. Also the order to the actors and cameraperson or technicians to stop action.

Dailies or Rushes: Film is processed the same day it is shot, then reviewed by the production staff either on the evening of the shoot day or the next evening.

Day Player: A principal performer hired on a daily basis, rather than on a longer-term contract.

Dealer Spot: A national commercial produced and paid for by a national advertiser and then turned over to local dealers to book airtime, usually with a dealer's tag added on.

Deferred Payment: An agreement to work without payment with the understanding that payment will be delayed, not waived, until the project generated income. Deferred payment must be approved by the union before the work begins.

Dissolve: Action fades out of one scene into another.

Dolly: Camera movements forward and backward, usually on tracks.

Double: Any performer who performs in place of another player.

Double Time: Double the straight time pay that is payable for certain overtime hours defined in each contract.

Downgrade: To hire a performer as a principal and move him or her to a lower category. When a performer is engaged as a principal but her or his voice or face does not remain in the final cut commercial, the performer must be notified that s/he has been downgraded. This means no residuals will be forthcoming, but the actor will receive one additional session fee. Performers should always call the union or agent for clarification if a downgrade occurs.

DP: Director of Photography.

Dress the Set: Add items to the set such as curtains, furniture, pictures, props, and so forth.

8 × 10:   Size of photo commonly used for headshots, portrait shots, composites.

Establishing Shot: A wide camera shot that orients the audience as to the location.

Executive Producer: Person or persons in the company responsible for funding the production.

Exteriors: Scenes for TV or motion pictures taken outdoors or using outdoor sets in a studio.

Extra: Non-principal role, used as background. Also called Atmosphere or Background.

ECU or Extreme Close-Up: Very tight shot of a subject (an actor's eye, a dog's teeth).

Field Rep: AFTRA or SAG staff member who goes to the set to ensure that contractual agreements are being met.

First Refusal: This is a request by a producer to hold a particular date open for a job. If you receive another job offer for that date, tell the second producer you are on first refusal and you'll get back to him or her. Then call the first producer and ask if s/he is going to use you since you have another offer for that day. If the first producer says "Yes," you are booked for the first job. If the first producer says "No," you can take the second booking. If you have an agent, s/he will do all this for you.

First Team: In movies, the stars and principals; actors with lines.

Fixed Cycle: For commercials, an established thirteen-week period for which the advertiser pays a holding fee to retain the right to use the commercial. The first fixed cycle starts with your session date.

Four-A's: Associated Actors and Artists of America; an umbrella organization for AFTRA, SAG, and other performers' unions.

Freelancer: An actor who has not signed a contract with an agent and who represents him/herself in getting auditions, negotiating terms of contracts, and other transactions.

Gaffer: In film, a crew member who places lighting instruments.

"Give me a level":   The sound person will request this of the performer in order to adjust sound equipment for proper audio recording. It means to start speaking the way you'll speak when actually performing.

Glossy: A shiny photofinishing process; also a term used to mean an 8 × 10 photo.

Golden Time: Overtime beginning with the sixteenth hour when an extra performer receives the full-day rate for each hour worked on commercial, television, and theatrical contracts.

Grip: A crew member who moves set pieces or props.

Headshot (also Headsheet):   A photo, usually 8 × 10, of the actor's head and shoulders.

Hold: A hold is the same as a booking. It is an offer of employment, a verbal contract, and is binding. Some people use the term as if it meant "first refusal," which is inappropriate. If unsure, always ask: "Do you mean that I am firmly booked for this job on this date?"

Holding Fee: This fee is paid to the actor, and it gives the producer the right to hold and show the commercial in which an actor appears. The holding fee is the same amount as one session fee (unless otherwise negotiated) and is paid at the beginning of each thirteen-week period (called a cycle) for as long as the commercial is being held by the agency or producer. The session fee covers the first thirteen-week holding fee.

Honey Wagon: A towed vehicle containing one or more dressing rooms and/or craft services.

IATSE: International Alliance of Theatrical Stage Employees. A union representing crew and technical employees.

Improvisation ("Improv"): Actors are given a situation by the director, and they create dialogue and actions. Frequently done in auditions when there is no actor copy for a commercial. Additional fees may be required under various contracts.

Industrial: Nonbroadcast, often educational films or tapes, designed for in-house use by a company. Also called Corporate Video.

"In" Time: An actor's call or start time; also return time from lunch or dinner break.

"Lay it down": Record or film the material.

Long Shot (LS): A camera shot that captures the actor's whole body.

Looping (also called Automatic Dialogue Replacement, or ADR): In a recording studio, the performer watches film (usually of him/herself) and simultaneously records dialogue so that it is in sync with the moving lips on the screen.

Major Markets: Large cities where the majority of work takes place. Los Angeles and New York are the two largest.

Mark: The spot, usually indicated by tape, where an actor is assigned to stand.

Master Shot: A wide camera shot of the complete scene, to be intercut with close-ups or other shots.

Maximum Use Period: The period of time (twenty-one months/seven cycles) that a producer may use a commercial without further negotiation. It is the actor's responsibility to notify the producer before the end of the maximum use period (120 to 60 days before the end of the use period) that s/he wishes to renegotiate. If notice is not given, the producer automatically retains the right to renew the commercial for another twenty-one months at the same rate. Contact your local union office or agent for specifics on procedure.

Meal penalty: A set fee paid by the producer for failure to provide meals or meal breaks at the time specified by the contract.

Medium Close-Up (MCU):   A shot that is not as tight as a close-up.

Medium Shot (MS):   A closer shot than a long shot. If the long shot took in an entire room, the MS might be half the room.

MOS (Mit Out Sound):   Any shot without dialogue or sound.

Multicamera: More than one camera used during filming.

NABET: National Association of Broadcast Employees and Technicians. A union representing crew and technical employees.

National Commercial: A commercial aired nationwide.

Night Premium: A percentage surcharge for work performed between 8:00 P.M. and 6:00 A.M.

Off-camera (OC or OS or Voice-over):   Dialogue delivered without being on screen.

Open Call: An audition or interview situation open to anyone.

Outgrade: The performer shoots a commercial and is paid a session fee. His/her work isn't used in the final commercial. The producer has the right to outgrade, which means no residuals will be paid to the performer.

"Out" Time: The time after which you have changed out of wardrobe and are released.

Overtime (OT):   Work extending beyond eight hours.

PA: Production assistant. Worker on a set who does whatever is assigned to her/him. Could be directing traffic, rounding up extras, keeping onlookers out of the picture, and so on.

Pan: Camera shot that sweeps from one side to the other.

Paymaster: An independent talent payment company that provides a payroll service for signatories and acts as the employer of record. For the industrial contract, the paymaster may also be the signatory.

Pension and Health (or Health and Retirement) Payment: An amount of money paid by the employer to cover actor health and pension benefits. Contributions are in addition to gross pay and are based on a percentage of the actor's gross salary.

Per Diem: Set fee paid by producer who hires out-of-town actors for location shoots; this compensates for expenditures for meals not provided by the producer.

Pickup: A scene is filmed and the director feels part of it is unusable. Rather than reshoot the whole scene, a pickup is done from the point where the work became unusable.

Postproduction: Everything that takes place on a TV show, movie, or commercial after shooting is done. Music, voice-over, sound effects, editing.

POV Shot: Point-of-view shot. Camera angle from the perspective of one actor.

Preproduction: Everything that takes place on a TV show, movie, or commercial before shooting begins. Casting, location scouting, script, and so forth.

Principal: An actor who is given a scripted line or lines or is asked to speak and is recorded during filming. Some contracts (industrial/commercial) also provide for performers to be paid as principals under other specific conditions.

Producer: Often called the Line Producer, the person responsible for the day-to-day decision-making on a production. Concerned with administrative details.

PSA: Public Service Announcement. A spot for a nonprofit organization, not-for-profit fund-raising event, or a charity. Actors are usually paid a session fee but no residuals for doing a PSA. A waiver must be granted by the union to the producer prior to employment.

Reaction Shot: A shot taken of an actor responding to another actor's lines or actions. Frequently done independently of the action.

Regional Commercial (or "Regional"):   A commercial produced for airing only in certain areas of the United States, not nationwide.

Released/Release Letter: When a client is not going to use or hold a commercial any longer, the actor is released. Notification by the producer is required.

Rerun: Rebroadcast of a TV program.

Residual: The fee paid to a performer for rebroadcast of a commercial, film, or TV program.

Resume: List of credits, usually attached to the back of an 8×10 headshot.

Reverse: Moving the camera to shoot from the other actor's point of view.

Run-through: Rehearsal.

SAG: Screen Actors Guild. Union for actors that represents performers appearing on film: movies, filmed TV shows, filmed commercials.

Scale: Minimum payment for services under union contracts.

Scale + 10 percent: Minimum payment plus 10 percent, generally charged to cover an agent's commission; required in some jurisdictions before agents can receive commissions.

Script Supervisor: The crew member assigned to record all changes or actions as the production proceeds.

Second Team: The stand-ins.

Session Fee: Payment for initial performance (the day or days you actually work) in a commercial.

Set: An indoor location, often constructed in a studio.

"Settle":   Term that the AD often uses to quiet everyone on the set in preparation for rolling the tape or film.

Setup: A camera shot with camera, lights, and so forth, placed in a specific way. When the camera, light, sound, etc. are moved to a different position or location, you have a new setup. Films/commercials are made in a series of setups.

SFX: Sound effects.

Sides: Pages or scenes from a script, used for auditions.

Signatory: An employer who has agreed to produce, under the terms of a union contract.

Silent Bit: Contract definition of this term: "Where an Extra Player is directed to and does satisfactorily rehearse or perform pantomime of such significance that it portrays a point essential to the staging of the scene involved . . . ." Whether an actor has performed a silent bit or not is at the discretion of the assistant director nearest the actor when the shot was being made. If in doubt, ask.

Slate: The process by which a performer identifies him/herself in a taped audition. The auditioner says, "Slate your name," and the performer looks into the lens of the camera and says who s/he is. Also, a small chalkboard and clapper device (called a clapboard or sticks) used when filming to make and identify each shot on film or tape for editing purposes.

"Speed":   Operators of film, video, or sound equipment say this to indicate equipment has reached the proper RPMs and is ready to record.

Spokesperson/Spokes: An on/off-camera performer speaking as him/herself directly to the viewing/listening audience.

Spot: Used to mean a commercial. "I did a spot for. . . ."

Standard Union Contract: The contract approved by AFTRA/SAG, completed by the producer and performer at the time of a shoot, and submitted for payment.

"Stand by":   Order to get ready to begin; it's given by the director, assistant director, or production assistants.

Stand-in: Extra player used to substitute for featured players, usually for the purpose of setting lights, camera blocking, and blocking the actor's physical action.

Storyboard: An artist's hand-drawn rendering of each camera setup in the commercial.

Studio: A building/room that accommodates film or TV production.

Submission: When an agent or casting director presents an actor's headshot to a producer for consideration for an audition or a role.

Taft-Hartley: A federal statute that allows thirty days after first employment before a performer is required to join a union.

Take: A scene or portion of a scene is usually filmed/taped more than once. A take is each time the camera rolls for a scene or portion of a scene.

Talent: Anyone who appears on-camera or whose voice is heard as voice-over.

Teleprompter: A device that scrolls a script in front of the lens, enabling the performer to read while appearing to know or to have memorized the material.

Test Market: Airing of a commercial in one geographical area to determine response.

Tight Shot: Framing of a shot with little or no space around the central figure(s) or feature(s); usually a close-up.

Theatrical: TV shows or feature film work, as opposed to commercials or non-broadcast productions.

Time-and-a-half: Hours nine and ten of a workday, during which time the performer receives one-and-a-half times the hourly rate under most contracts.

Trades: Trade papers; periodicals that carry entertainment information, such as *Back Stage* and *Variety*.

Turnaround: The number of hours between dismissal one day and call time the next day.

Two-shot: A shot in which two performers appear.

Upgrade: To hire a performer in one category, such as extra, and move her or him to a higher category. If an extra player is given a line, s/he is upgraded to principal.

Voice-over (VO/OS/OC):   Off-camera or off-screen voice work. The voice track produced separately, frequently in a sound studio.

Waiver: A waiver releases the producer from certain contractual situations. Only the union can approve a waiver.

Wardrobe: The clothing a performer wears on-camera.

Wardrobe Allowance: A maintenance fee paid to on-camera talent for the use and dry cleaning of talent's own clothing.

Wardrobe Fitting: When the producer is providing wardrobe, this is a paid session held prior to production to prepare a performer's costumes.

Wild Lines: An extra audio recording of lines said during on-camera filming/taping. In case any lines recorded with the camera have poor sound quality, wild lines can replace them during editing.

Wild Spot: A commercial that is contracted to air on a station-by-station basis, rather than on a network.

"Wrap":   Term used to indicate that the shooting for the day or for the production is finished.

Zoom: A camera technique with a special lens to adjust the depth of a shot without moving the camera.

Biography

Pat Dougan is an actor, teacher, trainer, and director. She has appeared in over 650 national and regional commercials, industrials, voice-overs, television shows, plays, and films since she started in the business in 1976. She costarred as Olympia Dukakis' daughter in the television drama *Rachel's Dinner,* appeared as a doctor with Nancy Marchand and Robert Urich in *Spenser: For Hire,* and was featured as an arbitrator with Michael O'Keefe in *Against the Law.*

Pat attended the Neighborhood Playhouse, where she studied acting with Sandy Meisner and later with Uta Hagen at HB Studio in New York.

Pat has been teaching on-camera acting for ten years. She teaches classes privately, and at Brandeis University in the Professional Theatre Training MFA Program. She has conducted classes and workshops at Salem State College, Boston University, and the North Shore Music Theatre.

Pat also teaches communication skills to lawyers, executives, managers, union representatives, insurance agents, public officials, and professional speakers, through workshops and one-on-one coaching.

A member of SAG, AFTRA, and AEA, Pat is a cofounder of StageSource, The Alliance of Theatre Artists and Producers in Boston, and was an AFTRA board member for six years.